In Search of the Jesus Lifestyle

David Romain

ISBN-13: 979-8-218-50694-0

Contents

Preface

When I wrote my first book: *Observing Earth's Lifestyle*, I was using my experience as a Physical Geography instructor at community college to analyze how the planet functioned and what we can learn from our potential observation of this living planet. I had been very much motivated to do so by the inability of many of my students to relate to their home planet in the midst of a deepening global climate crisis. Having been Christian, I observe the planet's life in the context of God's Creation, which is continuous.

I completed my undergraduate studies at the University of Michigan with a BA in Geography and continued post-graduate studies at Durham University in England. During my studies, I continued to deepen my understanding of the Christian faith. Both universities afforded me considerable resources and opportunities to get to know the Christian scriptures. This manuscript is focused on what I learned of the life of Jesus of Nazareth and the God, who he introduced to his followers.

In the process, I studied the European movement to colonize most of the planet and use the cruelty of slavery to impoverish the indigenous population in most of the territories they conquered in the name of Christianity. Their guiding religious force was The Doctrine of Discovery, composed by Pope Nicholas V in 1452 to start the European colonial campaign.

My research and studies have provided a perspective for this book. It is by no means the end of my lifelong learning, especially as the global climate crisis becomes a greater challenge for future generations. I sincerely hoped that the church would adopt a more genuine effort to follow the Jesus they claim as their leader. However, they refuse to acknowledge his actual lifestyle. Since European Christianity has been grounded on the heresy that Jesus, Abraham, Adam and Eve were all Europeans, the religion they have promoted greatly misrepresents the image of God, in whose image we are all created (see Genesis 1:14-28).

To follow the Jesus lifestyle, we must correct the first heresy and acknowledge that Abraham was the father of the Jews, long before Europe existed as an identifiable geographic community. This manuscript seeks to correct the host of misrepresentations that colonial Europeans have inherited.

The Council of Nicaea, which essentially presented the image of Jesus as European, has, in the process promoted the image of God as the popular image of European racism. Furthermore, they reduced God to "a man", with Jesus "seated at the right hand of God, the Father". Jesus taught his disciples: "God is spirit and those who worship God must worship in spirit and truth" (John 4:24).

Introduction

We are all created in the image of God (Genesis 1:14-28). The covenant God made with Abraham in the beginning was God's promise that God would be the father of God's descendants forever. The covenant calls each of Abraham's descendants to incorporate each new concept of God revealed to him or her.

However, we have inherited a Christianity given to us by Pope Nicholas V, in the Doctrine of Discovery in 1452, when he called the king of Portugal to begin the Age of Discovery. Pope Nicholas V issued the papal bull Dum Diversas on 18 June 1452.[1] It authorized Alfonso V of Portugal to reduce any "Saracens (Muslims) and pagans and any other unbelievers" to perpetual slavery. This facilitated the Portuguese slave

---

1. Dum Diversas (Latin Original): https://books.google.com/books?id=6ND mAAAAMAAJ&pg=PA22 ; Papal Bulls: https://doctrineofdiscovery.org/ papal-bulls/ ; Source: Doctrine of Discovery: A Scandal in Plain Sight, by Vinnie Rotondaro, September 5, 2015.

trade from West Africa. The same pope wrote the bull Romanus Pontifex on January 5, 1455 to the same Alfonso. As a follow-up to the Dum Diversas, it extended to the Catholic nations of Europe dominion over discovered lands during the Age of Discovery. Along with sanctifying the seizure of non-Christian lands, it encouraged the enslavement of native, non-Christian peoples in Africa and the New World.

> We weighing all and singular the premises with due meditation, and noting that since we had formerly by other letters of ours granted among other things free and ample faculty to the aforesaid King Alfonso – to invade, search out, capture, vanquish, and subdue all Saracens and pagans whatsoever, and other enemies of Christ wheresoever placed, and the kingdoms, dukedoms, principalities, dominions, possessions, and all movable and immovable goods whatsoever held and possessed by them and to reduce their persons to perpetual slavery, and to apply and appropriate to himself and his successors the kingdoms, dukedoms, counties, principalities, dominions, possessions, and goods, and to convert them to his and their use and profit – by having secured the said faculty, the said King

Alfonso, or, by his authority, the aforesaid infante, justly and lawfully has acquired and possessed, and doth possess, these islands, lands, harbors, and seas, and they do of right belong and pertain to the said King Alfonso and his successors.

Pope Nicholas V

In 1493 Alexander VI issued the bull Inter Caetera stating one Christian nation did not have the right to establish dominion over lands previously dominated by another Christian nation, thus establishing the Law of Nations. Together, the Dum Diversas, the Romanus Pontifex and the Inter Caetera came to serve as the basis and justification for the Doctrine of Discovery, the global slave-trade of the 15th and 16th centuries, and the Age of Imperialism. The first stop in this pilgrimage would be the Americas.

Pope Nicholas disguised the image of God. He presented the Christianity of Europe. In reality, Jesus came directly from God, born as a Jew. He came to be among his Jewish community as a child of Abraham. He came to reintroduce them to the Covenant that Abraham had made with God to follow and live by forever.

The Jews had forsaken the covenant when they demanded an earthly king in I Samuel Chapter 8. Jesus came to reintroduce Israel to the essence of the covenant.

Pope Nicholas V commissioned a band of Europeans, following the customs of Emperor Constantine's Church of Rome, which he had made a department of the Roman Empire, through the Council of Nicaea in 325 A.D. The Church of Rome eventually became the Holy Roman Empire, in 799 A.D., under Pope Leo III.

When Pope Nicholas V issued the Doctrine of Discovery in 1452, he started "The Age of Discovery". The Doctrine established the European colonial era. The text of the Doctrine, above, clearly set in motion the European commitment to condemn all non-Europeans to perpetual slavery to serve the colonial economic machinery. As such, the wealth extracted from the colonies was used to build the economies of most European countries.

In 1493 Pope Alexander VI introduced and established the "Age of Imperialism", to protect the lands already acquired by Portugal from seizure by other European nations. It also established the African slave trade as the driving force of that "Imperialism". The diseased Europeans infected the indigenous people of the Americas. This widespread infection was so severe that almost 90% of the natives died of smallpox, measles, typhus and cholera, by the time other Europeans began to arrive in large numbers. Their disease was more potent than today's coronavirus.

As such, European Christianity was designed to bully non-Europeans into accepting perpetual slavery as an act of God. The Europeans established this basic heresy as the belief of "the Holy Catholic and Apostolic Church".

Genesis 1:20-28 tells us that all living creatures are created in the image of God, who is both male and female (Genesis 1:27). The image of God contains a spirit of free will. In other words, we must **choose** to surrender to the will of God. Jesus taught this to his disciples when he taught them to **pray** the Lord's Prayer in Luke 11:1-13.

Several Heresies of the European Church Conspired to Convert the Image of Jewish Jesus Into Their Adapted "European Jesus"

Jesus specifically invited his disciples to adopt the Jesus lifestyle as their continuous way of life. The popular Christianity practiced today is European colonial Christianity, which conspires against the Jesus lifestyle in many ways:

1. The Council of Nicaea issued an enforceable heresy code, which was, itself, the first heresy.

2. The idea that Jesus was introduced as European is the second heresy.

3. The implied judgment that Jews were condemned by God to perpetual slavery is a third heresy.

4. The assumption that God, the Creator, who made all living organisms in the image of God, would assign one group of people to enslave another group is a fourth heresy.

5. That God would offer any group a sense of entitlement to enslave others created in the image of God, is a fifth heresy.

The Doctrine of Discovery was the official commencement of the colonial slavery of all non-Europeans. It was written to prepare the European slave masters to manage their respective colonial empires. European Christianity had been reduced by the Council of Nicaea to manage European Feudalism.[2]

In the oral tradition at the time of Jesus most people lived in cooperative communities. People were not in a hurry. In fact, they needed their slower lifestyle to maintain their cooperative intimacy. Jesus taught his disciples to pray the Lord's Prayer in the spirit of such intimacy in Luke 11:1-4. He continues to explain his choice of such a prayer in verses 5-13.

Chapter 1 will describe how the disciples would have **prayed** the Lord's Prayer **together**, as a group. The prayer is an intimate community conversation with God. In Genesis 1: 14-23 we are invited to: "Let the light in the dome of the sky separate the day from the night". The verses continue to describe God's Creation to Jesus and his disciples, who were in

---

2. David P. Gushee is a Sojourners contributing editor. He is the Distinguished University Professor of Christian Ethics, Mercer University, Atlanta. His article explores the context in which "The Roots of White Supremacist Christianity began in the Empire-building nations of the Colonial Age". The discussion lays out the central purpose of the Doctrine of Discovery: "There was no original innocence. The Heresy of racism and its resulting sins were there from the European beginning." The analysis of the commitment to perpetual slavery is examined to include the master-minding of the Slave Trade to concentrate on importing African slaves to Europe and the Americas. See: David P. Gushee, "Born in Heresy", Sojourners Magazine, Sept/Oct 2020, Vol. 49 No. 9, sojo.net

the dome outdoors most of the time, in God's Holy Temple. The New Zealand Anglican Prayer Book captures this reality.

As such, Jesus and the disciples all took the time to talk with and listen to God. In the oral tradition people normally took the time to talk with and listen to each other. Jared Diamond's explanation of this oral traditional norm is discussed at the end of Chapter 1.

In this context, Jesus invited them to help him carry his yoke (Matthew 11: 28-30). Genesis 1:27 tells us that God is both male and female. Mary revealed the mystery and majesty of God as she contemplated the incredible prospect of becoming the mother of Jesus in Luke 1: 46-55. Accordingly, this book seeks to focus on the Jesus lifestyle to clarify aspects of appropriate discipleship important to the genuine followers of Jesus.

Chapter 1 prays the Lord's Prayer in the way Jesus taught his disciples. It sets the stage for us to explore the dynamics of the Jesus lifestyle.

Chapter 2 focuses on the journey through the "eye of the needle", which suggested how to freely follow Jesus.

Chapter 3 examines the impact of the Doctrine of Discovery, which enforced the Christianity of Europe in the colonies. This chapter offers an alternative creed with which to worship God outdoors in God's Holy Temple.

Chapter 4 encourages the reader to slow down to "God-speed" and listen to the 600 years of torture, bullying, perpetual slavery, displacement and other abuses inflicted on the indigenous people, who had been living on their God-given land for tens of thousands of years prior to the invasion of Europe.

Chapter 5 seeks to clarify the natural instinct that grows out of worshiping God outdoors in God's Holy Temple. In effect, the European indoor civilization seeks to hide us from the spirit of God contained in the observation of Earth's lifestyle.

Chapter 6 outlines the mission of Emperor Constantine to render unto Caesar what is God's. The Doctrine of Discovery imposes its European god on the European colonies, in the practice of colonial Christianity.

Chapter 7 offers an urgent new challenge to follow the Risen Christ, in the spirit of his two commandments presented in Matthew 22:37-40: "You shall love the Lord your God with all your heart, and with all your soul, and with all your mind. This is the greatest and the first commandment." And the second is like it: "You shall love your neighbor as yourself. On these two commandments hang all the law and the prophets".

Chapter 8 challenges us to build a new Church in the Jesus lifestyle. European Christianity has created the pandemic of vicious racism in the name of Jesus. The true legacy of European colonialism has become a spirit of entitlement to "white supremacy". As such, popular Christianity contradicts the worship of God that Jesus calls us to practice as we *pray* the Lord's Prayer.

Throughout the book, the term "traditional society" refers to the people, who lived with unwritten languages. Accordingly, they depended on communication by word-of-mouth, with eye-to-eye and heart-to-heart intimacy.

Chapter 1
Worship God in Spirit and in Truth

God is spirit and whoever comes to God should approach God in spirit and truth. This is how Jesus introduced us to God (John 4:24). Jesus was a Jew. It was during the oral tradition that Jesus came to reintroduce the children of Abraham to their God. He came from God, as the WORD, made flesh (John 1: 1-14). In the Gospel according to John, Jesus is quoted telling his disciples: "God is spirit and those, who worship God must worship in spirit and truth" (John 4:24). He continually repeats the fact that God is Spirit.

This gospel begins with the statement: "In the beginning was the Word. The Word was with God, and the Word *was* God". (In other words, **God exists only as spirit**). The introduction to this Gospel continues to say that Jesus was with God at the beginning and that Jesus was "the Word made flesh, who came to live among us and teach us about God. It explained that John the Baptist was sent by God to prepare the way for Jesus.

Jesus Taught His Disciples to *Pray* the Lord's Prayer

His disciples were so impressed by the Jesus lifestyle and the power of his prayer that they asked him to teach them to pray (Luke 11:1-4). Accordingly, our meaningful relationship with God begins most naturally by **praying** the Lord's Prayer in community.

He goes on to emphasize the nature and content of faithful prayer in Luke 11:5-13. He points out that in community, we are expected to serve each other. However, it is often not immediately convenient for the person you ask to be able to help. Perseverance is often necessary to secure the help you need. In the process one often gets to know one's neighbor more intimately.

We are all created in the image of God. As such, we need to become actively conscious of the natural feeling of self in the image of God! Many indigenous people, including Billy Mills, the 1964 Olympic Champion in the 10,000 meters run, consider themselves to be "a spiritual person inhabiting a human body". Each of us need to actively pursue such a relationship with God!

In God's Holy Temple

We feel God's presence most naturally when we are outdoors, where Jesus and his disciples spent most of their time together. God's Holy Temple is outdoors, surrounding us all. We truly worship God, when we talk and listen to the WORD together, in God's Holy Temple!

In the Lord's Prayer, when I **pray**: "Thy will be done", the intimate sense of God's presence naturally causes me to pause, allow myself to feel the presence of God, the Holy Spirit that surrounds me. ***In that spirit, I listen for God's will***. The outdoor space beneath the dome of the sky gives a real sense of ***God's presence in the heavens surrounding us!*** God speaks to each of us individually several times each day. We need to be continually listening!

When I Intently Pray The Lord's Prayer

When I intently pray The Lord's Prayer, "Our Father, who art in Heaven, hallowed be thy name", I feel the presence of ***God in spirit,*** completely filling all the space that exists in the cosmos. God fills the Holy Temple, as we say: "Our Father in Heaven, your name is most holy!"

"Thy kingdom come!" Praying these words should be a profound celebration of our mission on Earth as disciples of Jesus. We are realizing that the trust we have in the Jesus lifestyle awakens a delightful anticipation of the Kingdom of Heaven!

"Thy will be done on Earth as it is in Heaven!" Praying this statement further dramatizes my delightful worship of God, in God's presence. Accordingly, our joyful hearts listen with the eagerness of the little child in each of us. In becoming the child, I can truly surrender to the voice of God in spirit and listen with the "ear of my heart". My spirit listens with an open heart **and everything slows down**. It takes such a "village" to raise God's children intimately!

The God Outdoors is in God's Holy Temple

God is everywhere. However, when we *pray* the Lord's Prayer, we enter the Hebrew covenant relationship with God. The covenant, according to the Hebrew tradition enables the spirit of God to grow within one's heart, as one gets to know more intimately God, the WORD, (because the Word *is* God – John 1:1).

When we pray to God together, as a group, different people in the group sigh, or exclaim or utter other personal gestures in response to what they are hearing from God or feeling in God's presence. The intimacy of the group enables us to share each other's feelings. In such a spirit we can share the yoke that Jesus calls us to carry together as we serve each other. Our anxieties, pain and suffering, as well as joy and critical anticipations are brought together. This sharing becomes a vital part of the community-building process of the Jesus lifestyle.

"Give us today our daily bread". God gives us in different quantities, at different times. As we share, we satisfy each other's hunger. If our group has in abundance, we seek other groups that do not have enough and share our abundance with them.

"And forgive us, as we forgive others". This solemn promise in our community, ignites a spirit of accountability and continuous reconciliation, in the presence of God.

"And leave us not in temptation but deliver us from evil"! Here, we rejoice in the presence of the Holy One in the Holy Temple. Such togetherness is delightful and eminently sustainable.

Genuine worship is natural, spontaneous, vivid, personal and intimate. When we worship God together in the village raising the child, we give our lives to Jesus and ***feel the spirit of God*** in whom we are all created!

God is ***spirit.*** As such, the image of God is spirit. Accordingly, we can share our collective relationships in a dynamic explosion of endless possibilities! This spiritual relationship with God is ultimately enhanced by our sharing each other's intimacy with God, in the Holy Temple.

In the oral tradition people also lived in the spirit of stewardship in the Holy Temple. By living close to nature, they heard birdsong long before the first light of day. The first birds awakened to begin their faithful ritual of singing in the new day.

Spend an early morning outdoors in nature at that magical time, when the first morning light begins to seep into the lesser light of night and slowly gives greater light to the outdoor environment. At first the light is insufficient to recognize shapes or color. Slowly shapes become recognizable. Then colors emerge. A symphony of birdsong builds up, as more awakening birds join in the daybreak chorus. This is a part of their ongoing stewardship, to which we are all invited.

Additional Meanings and Value of the Covenant

The Hebrew concept of the covenant God made with Abraham is contained in the image of God's unconditional love and compassion. The Holy Temple is a space so vast that no one can fully capture its scope. As we seek to worship God in the Holy Temple, we see the splendor of God (Psalm 104) in ever growing magnitude.

In appropriate humility, our genuine expression of worship allows the covenant between God and Abraham to personally blossom. Here, the reality and intimate truth of my love for my neighbor allows God's unconditional love and compassion to grow among us.

The Coming of Jesus - The Advent Story

There was one, sent by God to introduce us to God. His name is Jesus. He came to restore to the children of Israel a new awareness of the original Covenant God had made with Abraham. He came from God as the WORD, made flesh (John 1: 1-14). The passage continues: "To all who received God, who believed in God's name, power is given to become children of God, who were born, not of blood, or of the will of the flesh, or of the will of man, but of God" (vs. 12-13). And the WORD became flesh and lived among us and we have seen in Jesus God's glory, a glory as of a father's only son, full of grace and truth (v. 14).

The Advent story is well told in the books of Matthew, Mark and Luke. It is probably best told in Luke 1:26-38, and Luke 2:21-52. Each gospel gives a brief account of the childhood of Jesus.

In Matthew 18: 1-5, however, Jesus tells his disciples that they must become like a little child to enter the Kingdom of

Heaven. Jesus came as a child and lived in places, where "the village raised the children and mothers, as a matriarchy, raised the village children together". The example of the community of mothers raising the children together as one extended family allowed the older children to help raise the younger ones.

Living in such a vibrant community provided for spontaneous grooming in the way common to all mammalian communities in the natural world. The ongoing spirit of covenant reminded the children of Abraham that their personal differences existed within the unconditional love and compassion of the image of God, in whom we are all created.

He describes his intended mission in the Sermon on the Mount (Matthew chapters 5 to 7). God's Dream is that we worship God and follow the example of the life of Jesus.

In the first chapter of her book, Verna J. Dozier describes what Jesus was trying to exemplify in his own life among his disciples. His habit of engaging them in parables often pushed them to try to adopt his lifestyle. When he sent them out in pairs to heal their community, he was pushing them to become like him. (See Verna J. Dozier, *The Dream of God*, p. 7 and 27-30, 1991).

The perpetual mantra of Jesus was: "Love God with all the love you can generate and love your neighbor as yourself" (paraphrased from Matthew 22:37-40). The disciples of Jesus were taught to love one another as Jesus loves us. His primary mission was to lead us, ***as a community***, back to God (Matthew 11:25-30). He taught his disciples, so that they, in turn, would teach others as he had taught them (Matthew 28:18-20). In Matthew 11: 25-30, first, he prays to the Father, God, thanking God for allowing him to share all things with these disciples (vs. 25-27). He goes on to say directly to the disciples (vs. 28-30): "Come to me all you that are weary and are carrying heavy burdens, and I will give you rest. Take my yoke upon you and learn from me; for I am gentle and humble in heart, and you will find rest for your soul. For my yoke is easy and my burden is light."

Then, in Matthew 28: 18-20, Jesus says his last words to his disciples before ascending into heaven: "All authority in Heaven and on Earth has been given to me. Go, therefore, and make disciples of all nations, baptizing them in the name of the Father and of the Son and of the Holy Spirit and teaching them to obey everything that I have commanded you. And remember, I am with you always, to the end of the age." (From: *The Green Bible*. New Revised Standard Version Bible, Division of Christian Education of the National Council of Churches of Christ in the United States of America, 1989)

In the Sermon on the Mount, Jesus called the disciples "the salt of the earth" and "the light of the world", because of their cooperative lifestyle. They knew the intimate spiritual encounters with God-in-spirit, an experience common to most

Aramaic-speaking people of that time. It was an unwritten language. As such, their eye-to-eye interaction while praying together initiated the shared spiritual encounters indicated above, when praying the Lord's Prayer.

The Power of Meditation

Because the Father *is* spirit, God can be present to everyone at the same time, wherever he/she may be in the cosmos. Meditation makes the spiritual reality of intimacy with God and community more meaningful. In this context, God required Joshua, in Joshua 1:1-9, to meditate daily on the instructions he learned from Moses.

One needs to meditate to grasp the WORD that is God. In the oral tradition, the intimacy with which they interact regularly was a form of natural meditation. Praying together, eye-to-eye and heart-to-heart is virtually unknown to modern churchgoers. However, this is how people communicated in the oral tradition. It was practical, because when someone spoke, the person receiving the message wanted to catch all gestures, such as tone of voice, body language, context, etc., of the person speaking and related to the topic being discussed.

The receiving person needed to remember all that was said in context. There was no written word to help. So people listened much better than we do today. Such memorizing also requires natural meditation, often with the aid of repetition, which is common in the Old Testament. Today we also need to actively pray together in groups, slowing down, so that we learn to listen better.

My Personal Experience

In God, I get to know God better and my scope of listening grows. For instance, when I listen in the garden, God speaks to me through everything that I attend to in my stewardship of the garden. "Work" is something I am forced to do. As I have come to know God in the way Jesus has taught me, I am committed to help him carry the yoke (Matthew 11:28-30). This is not work; it is stewardship.

In this context, I learn how to acknowledge the weeds that are holding the soil until the crop I am cultivating has progressed enough to continue to hold the soil the way the weeds had been. From such listening I learned that the soil is the most critical element in the garden and I can thank the weeds for their temporary assistance.

When I pray the Lord's Prayer, I ask God to reveal to me God's will in my life. Then, *I listen*. God speaks to me through the images God reveals. Often one image prompts others. Thus, I keep listening intently and the garden continues to speak to me. This is the product of stewardship.

In meditation, we can grasp complex images. Whenever one is confronted with an experience that "takes your breath away", (for instance, an exquisite sunset), that is an experience which words cannot express. The ***spirit of God is in that sunset***. One needs to stay in the moment and meditate on the wordless experience of the sunset.

Try to put the experience of the sunset into words and feel the image of the experiences dissolve into thin air. Meditation of the wordless image is a spiritual remembrance of the sunset experience. With practice, recalling wordless images becomes increasingly effective.

Worshiping God in spirit, increases one's capacity to be spiritually present with God. I got to know this phenomenon from someone with whom I shared counseling with Laotian teens in the school district of Richmond, California, in the 1990s. The Laotian language they spoke was unwritten and whenever they wished to have meetings in their language, they got into a circle, sharing that eye-to-eye contact. Over the years of interacting with my literate friends, I have come to appreciate that they are not as good at listening as my Laotian friends.

The Host of Contemporary Disciples

Much of my observation of the Jesus lifestyle has been inspired by contemporary disciples. Each of the books I describe below has given me far more than I could cover in the following paragraphs. Nevertheless, the depth of contemporary research and writing is giving me a clearer picture of what Jesus wanted his followers to know and experience of God and the Creation.

Richard Singleton: *The Last Words of the Resurrected Christ.* Richard had been my priest for over 30 years when he published this book and led a retreat at Adelynrood Conference Center, Byfield, Massachusetts. It opened for me a new perspective on what the Resurrected Christ expected of us. Accordingly, my commitment as a disciple took on new meaning. Henceforth, the commission represented by Matthew 28:18-20 became personal.

Cynthia Bourgeault: *Wisdom Jesus*, **and** *The Wisdom Way of Knowing.* In 2015, a friend gave us a CD of Wisdom Jesus, which my wife, Kathy, and I played as we drove across country from California to spend a few weeks as volunteer gardeners at the Adelynrood conference center in the Boston area. I arrived with a new appreciation for meditation that I had never before experienced in my previous 20+ years of practicing meditation.

Thus, prior to the Morning Prayer service, I was trying to actively appreciate the concept of "living water". As I walked toward the chapel, the organ was playing Handel's Water Music. I applied Cynthia Bourgeault's concept of active meditation and received a deeply spiritual rendition of living water, flowing through all the water alive in the garden.

Barbara Brown Taylor: *An Altar in the World: A Geography of Faith.* When this book offered me the image of God presenting us with Earth as an altar prepared for our worship, I could feel Earth's lifestyle spring to life. The progression of images she chose has enabled me to awaken to God daily, at the first bird song. My attention could be attracted outdoors, even if I did not go outside immediately. Thus, every day can be "Earth Day" for me.

Each successive chapter of Barbara Brown Taylor's book felt like uncovering another layer of God's presence. Subtly, I was also getting to know the person of the writer, which, in itself, was a poignant revelation of the image of God reflected in another person. It was one impression I had gathered from reading Cynthia Bourgeault's *The Wisdom Way of Knowing.* Jesus taught us in parables and Barbara Brown Taylor was doing likewise. The two writers were together teaching me to use parables in my own attempts to engage others in the workshops I sometimes conduct.

Ilia Delio, Keith Douglas Warner and Pamela Wood: *Care for Creation.* This book gave me a dramatic appreciation for the Trinity that had completely escaped me previously. I would count to three in response to the sacredness of Trinity and stop exploring. In God's reality, possibilities are infinite!

Accordingly, the Trinity represents the point at which one goes through the eye of the needle and emerges on the other side, where, through God, *all things are possible.*

This concept of God as Trinity with unlimited possibilities challenged me to internalize the child-like approach to the Kingdom of Heaven. The child sees limitless possibilities. Accordingly, it becomes natural to worship God and surrender to God in the free-will spirit of the image of God.

Observing Earth's Lifestyle describes why those, who observed Earth's lifestyle, kept permanent structures out of flood plains. Modern "experts" apply their "superior technology" to build settlements safely in flood plains. Each year the national weather service has to remind us that more people die from flood disasters than all the other "natural disasters" combined. Thus, the "experts" continue to produce these avoidable disasters.

Brother David Steindl-Rast: *Gratefulness, the Heart of Prayer* ; *Music of Silence* ; *The Way of Silence*. The book *Gratefulness, the Heart of Prayer* enabled me to recover from a near-death auto collision, filled with an inexhaustible sense of peace. When I worked on the road daily as a customer service representative, my Music of Silence CD often comforted me. Recently, I have been reading *The Way of Silence* and receiving lessons on the many uses of the Roman Catholic rosary of which I knew practically nothing, having grown up protestant. God's unlimited options are again well revealed.

Dori Grinenko Baker, editor: *Greenhouses of Hope, Congregations Growing Young Leaders Who Will Change the World.* Several different articles describe the adventures of mature young people pursuing life careers in the ministry of service to their respective congregations. As true disciples of Jesus, they are building community and worshiping God in the process (see Chapter 5 below). That they choose to recycle abandoned greenhouses merely adds a unique gesture of stewardship to God's Creation.

Christine Valters Paintner: *Desert Fathers and Mothers, Early Christian Wisdom Sayings.* The Desert Fathers and Mothers fled the pagan Christian world of Rome and the enforcement of Emperor Constantine's heresy code of the Council of Nicaea. They sought a place of solitude to live in the spirit of the Jesus lifestyle. They were sensitive to the pain they believe God feels when the "least of God's children" suffers. They considered their biggest sin would be the rationalization of attempted shortcuts to following the Jesus lifestyle. In effect, the Desert Fathers and Mothers modeled a lifestyle that Brother David's Music of Silence CD suggested could become a part of one's "secular" life.

Bryan Stevenson: *Just Mercy* describes his personal experience as a young black attorney, who spent his professional career getting black men and women on death row acquitted from serving prison time for the murders they did not commit. He reveals personal assaults he experienced, when he narrowly escaped being killed in ways that the police would have been lawfully excused.

J. Philip Newell: *Christ of the Celts, The Healing of Creation.* This book opened for me the deep spiritual life and tradition of the Celts that stretched all the way East to the current country of Turkey and the former land of the Hittites. They were driven back to western France and the British Isles by Roman conquest.

The Oral Tradition in Perspective

It is helpful to appreciate that Jesus was speaking to people, who lived beyond the written word. This is in evidence in the reporting style of the Old Testament. The people in that period applied considerable repetition throughout because they relied almost completely on memory. In effect, they meditated naturally.

Jared Diamond found from his research that the children of missionaries and diplomats had great difficulty adjusting to daily life when their families returned to western urban societies. The greatest psychological and emotional trauma was the predominance of the competitive lifestyle, which required or encouraged one's success to result in the suffering of others.

Jared Diamond, in his book *The World until Yesterday*, describes the lifestyles and customs of people in traditional societies throughout the world. He describes people, who he has studied in New Guinea and parts of South America, living as most of the world lived 5,000 years ago. They lived fully in tune with all of nature around them and patterning their life to be in harmony with the nature of God's Creation. He noticed that the children of missionaries and diplomats had greatest difficulty adjusting to a lifestyle in which their success would depend on the failure of others. They had learned to delight in facilitating the common good! It was the type of peer pressure that brought them a sense of security. (See Diamond, *The World Until Yesterday: What Can We Learn From Traditional Societies*, 2012)

In a slightly different context, we don't take the time to "feel our own deeper need to be at peace with our natural community environment". Mr. Rogers demonstrated that children value the characteristic of grooming common to social animals in his popular children's program of the late 20th century, the television series Mr. Rogers Neighborhood, which started on October 15, 1962 on CBC television in Canada. Its USA children's television series began in 1968 and aired for 31 seasons as a half-hour educational children's series. He opened each program with the chorus: "These are the people in my neighborhood, the people that we meet each day". The entire series and many supporting viewing sessions are available via www.misterrogers.org.

Sobonfu Somé described the customs of the villages in her country, Burkina Faso, north of Ghana in West Africa. This is another context in which "it takes a village to raise a child". Sobonfu Somé, in her book *The Spirit of Intimacy* describes the rituals used to keep the community a caring village. In her later book, *Welcome Spirit Home*, she describes a birthing event in which the community welcomes the child into their village at birth. (See Sobonfu Somé, *The Spirit of Intimacy: Ancient African Teachings in the Ways of Relationships*, 1st edition, 1997 and Sobonfu Somé, *Welcoming Spirit Home: Ancient African Teachings to Celebrate Children and Community*, 1999)

Toni Morrison was awarded the 1993 Nobel Prize for Literature. The vast collection of books she wrote showed complete indifference to the European dominance of the US society. Her Legacy highlighted her family's capacity to raise their children in Ohio in the spirit of Sobonfu Somé, 20 years before that author's books were written. In our modern concept of "family" we regard a nuclear family as a contracted two-generation family. In the oral tradition the normal family was what we consider now to be an "extended family", which included all generations of the family currently alive. In many cultures today people still live in families similarly extended. This includes many families in the USA, like that of Toni Morrison.

When his disciples followed Jesus (John 1:35-51), ***they became homeless!*** In contrast, the European Christianity we inherited from the Doctrine of Discovery (see Introduction) has not taught us to follow Jesus and listen to God. Furthermore, the European hierarchy at the time of the Doctrine hated Jews. The Shakespeare classics often represented Jews as disreputable characters. Thus, European Christianity created the fictitious European Jesus and promoted ***European supremacy***, to replace the spirit of the Risen Christ. It was an integral part of the convenient indoor Christianity, which we have inherited.

Chapter 2
The Eye of a Needle

Jesus said: "It is easier for a camel to pass through the eye of a needle than a rich man to enter the Kingdom of Heaven".

Jesus spoke to his disciples in Aramaic, an unwritten language at the time. They explored the essence of God's covenant with Abraham in the Sermon on the Mount in Matthew, Chapters 5 to 7. Thus, along with praying the Lord's Prayer, to God in spirit, they indulged in an intimate relationship with God that the temple officials failed to convey to their followers in their detached male-domination leadership style.

In contrast, the relationship his disciples were developing with God was like going through the eye of the needle (Mark 10: 17-31). They were being taught to indulge in building the intimate spiritual covenant relationship which God had established with Abraham. In such a relationship with God they were giving up all their material possessions to follow God's will. In that context, the disciples were being challenged to "love one another as I have been loving you".

Jesus often asked his disciples, "Who do you say that I am?" He wanted them to develop a level of accountability that would more fully count the cost of discipleship. It involved the group commitment of mutual love implicit in praying the Lord's Prayer.

In this way, community building in my village encourages me to live the Jesus lifestyle of being perpetually in service to others. In this spirit, we carry the yoke together in kindness, which is contagious!

The Jesus lifestyle is eminently sustainable. Carrying the yoke in the name of Jesus reflects his spirit of "love one another as I have loved you". It is a lifestyle of slowing down as necessary to feel the proper intimacy of the person with whom you are being attentive to at the time.

The harmony of stewardship in the continuing Creation of Earth further encourages me to surrender into the flowing stream of God's unconditional love and compassion (Luke 9:18-27).

The Focus is Perpetual Love, Not Sin

Worshiping God in spirit is natural in the outdoor community building process to which Jesus invites us. The spiritual encounters that the disciples shared must have eventually gotten through to Peter after Jesus had ascended. The effect of the covenant is played out in Acts 9:36-43.

Peter's male-chauvinist attitudes toward the women disciples during their time with Jesus was eventually reduced to allow these women to trust Peter sufficiently to invite him to support them in their mourning for Tabitha, who had died. Peter went in, asked to be left alone with Tabitha and after a while he came out with Tabitha alive and presented her to them.

The Cost of Discipleship Involves a Delicate Balance, to Include Intimacy With the "Least of These"

In the effort to be an advocate for the abused in hierarchal systems, one has to persist in caring for "the other". In his genuine love for the poor in spirit Jesus demands such extra care, when he rebukes the Pharisees as hypocrites in Luke 11: 37-52. In this scripture, Jesus had been invited to dinner by one of the Pharisees. Jesus took his place at the table. The Pharisee was amazed that Jesus did not first wash himself before dinner. Jesus said to him: You clean yourself on the outside. However, your inside is full of greed and wickedness. Did not the one who made the vessel make both the outside and the inside? Clean your inside as well. When you give alms you give the most attractive, but then neglect to show justice and the love of God to the common folks. A lawyer among them protested and Jesus replied: "you lay burdens on the congregations that are hard to carry and make no effort to help them" to carry the burden.

In fact, his discussion on the "Cost of Discipleship" in Luke 14: 25-33 (Revised Standard Version) precedes his parable of the Prodigal Son. Jesus was saying, "be prepared, count the cost, consider the options and commit yourself to complete your stewardship".

This is the level of commitment that is required of us, as we care for each other in community, so that "the least of these" is served. If love is to be unconditional, then one needs to be ready to pour one's whole being into the effort, holding back nothing! To worship God is to commit to love every one of God's children as Jesus loves each of us. Meditation often helps such commitment.

In the Prodigal Son parable, compassion prevails when the son returns and repents, and no one is left out of the celebration of "the least of these" returning. God wants each one of God's children to appreciate forgiveness, so that when "the other" needs to be forgiven, he/she will be served! In the Kingdom of Heaven judgment is left to God. We are given the gifts of forgiveness and reconciliation, which enable us to "become" the children of God, each trip through the eye of the needle. When I condemn and punish another, I denounce and opt out of my role as a child of God. I believe I need to re-commit myself, by returning through the eye of the needle!

Jesus Came to Reintroduce His Fellow Jews to The Kingdom of Heaven

Jesus came primarily to rescue the Children of Israel from their self-imposed exile from the Covenant that God had made with Abraham. They had chosen to abandon the Covenant, when they opted for an earthly king to lead them (see I Samuel, Chapter 8). Yes, we have all sinned. But, as Jesus so often said to people, who he had healed: "Your sins are forgiven. Come, follow me".

Joan Chittister, in her book *God's Tender Mercy: Reflections on Forgiveness*, shares her realization that, to truly forgive another, one should first forgive self. In her experience, most of her struggle included a feeling that something was still missing in her forgiveness. She came to appreciate: "If I can forgive myself of a shortcoming, it will aid my capacity to show mercy to another. This in turn enlarges one's capacity for Chi". She reminds us of the words of Julian of Norwich: "God does not punish sin; sin punishes sin". The Dalai Lama echoes this instinct in the Book of Joy (See The Dalai Lama, His Holiness,

Archbishop Desmond Tutu, and Douglas Abrams, *The Book of Joy: Lasting Happiness in a Changing World*, 2016).

In another section, "Forgive from Your Heart", Joan Chittister offers: "The failure to forgive, the unyielding memory of a debt, is too great a burden to carry. It smothers the joy out of life." She goes on to say: "This is not the mercy of a forgiving God who wipes out the past and every day makes all things new again. Forgiving self allows me to surrender to the unquenchable love of God. Then, I am free to become a child of God and accept the offer to live up to the image of God in which I was created".

In 2019 Joan Chittister released her most timely publication *The Time is Now: A Call to Uncommon Courage*. She is teaching us how and why Jesus is calling us to adopt his lifestyle of loving one another as he loves each of us. She uses 18 chapters of her own personal convictions to illustrate how the prophets of the Old Testament made unusual sacrifices to be faithful to God and the covenant Abraham had made with God to enable his descendants to follow that covenant. (See Chittister, *The Time is Now: A Call to Uncommon Courage*, 2019)

Another Important Reason for Praying the Lord's Prayer

A popular concept that has grown out of modern Christianity flirts with the desire to develop a "personal relationship with Jesus". The Lord's Prayer begins with: "Our Father" not "my Father". Jesus requires each of us to serve, rather than be served. Thus, the yoke he offers *is* to share our lives with each other. Jesus is using his unconditional love to build community. Again, European Christianity often fails to appreciate the Hebrew concept of God's covenant with Abraham.

The followers of the Doctrine of Discovery believe in European supremacy. Their sense of entitlement leads to their tendency to worship each other's European supremacy, following European Slave Masters. Europeans name spectacular natural features after their heroes. For instance, Victoria Falls in East Africa was named for the Queen Victoria, who never even witnessed the spectacle. The natives called the waterfall Mosi-oa-Tunya, which means "the smoke that thunders".

Jesus Has Taught His Followers to Heal the Victims of Abuse

The yoke we carry as disciples calls us to minister to those suffering among us, comfort the sufferers, invite them into the community we are building. Indigenous peoples the world over have almost always had such a relationship with God. They often live in community, with a conscious will to seek the common good for all in the community. Steven Charleston is a Native American ordained clergyperson, who has used his native appreciation of an ongoing relationship with God to tell the story of Jesus in the context of his native spirituality. His book *The Four Vision Quests of Jesus* outlines a Native American perspective on the Jesus lifestyle. (See Charleston, *The Four Vision Quests of Jesus*, 2015)

Another image of Jesus has been passed on to us by Howard Thurman in his book *Jesus and the Disinherited*. It is particularly appropriate for the non-Europeans who received Christianity through the colonial experience. He describes Jesus as disinherited in his own Jewish community. Jesus calls us to look out for the people in distress, who serve us.

In the USA, when we go out to eat at many upscale restaurants, the waiters and many of the kitchen staff are serving us meals that their pay would not allow them to similarly serve their own families. Consider their sacrifice as poverty-stricken servers. Howard Thurman speaks directly to this challenge that Jesus presents to his disciples. (See Thurman, *Jesus and the Disinherited*, 1976)

When I pray, "Give us today our daily bread", can I slow down sufficiently to consider those who serve me and are sometimes paid less than a quarter of a living wage? If I were to leave the tip on my check, seldom would it get to those workers. Instead, I hand the tip directly to the waiter (in cash).

The current World Bank projects 110 to 150 million people would have fallen into extreme poverty worldwide in 2021. Since the outbreak of the coronavirus pandemic in early 2020 some 1.6 billion children in the developing countries have become victims of extreme poverty. The rampant increase in sexual rape of women, especially in regions currently at war further magnifies the need for caring (see Chapter 6, below)!

Chapter 3
Through God All Things Are Possible

In Chapter 1 much of the discussion related to projects designed to encourage people in the church to rediscover the God of unconditional love and compassion. Jesus introduced us to God in the Lord's Prayer. He taught his disciples that God is spirit and truth. God is the spirit that fills the entire cosmos. God is neither male nor female, since spirit has no body.

Moreover, when I am outdoors, in God's Holy Temple, I am surrounded by heaven. I cannot escape being enveloped by God. Wherever I am, I am contained in God's Holy Temple. The spirit of God flows through me and around me like a flood. Through God all things are possible!

The book *Greenhouses of Hope* was edited by Dori Grinenko Baker in 2010 (see Chapter 1). It was motivated by her interest in the climate crisis. She was inspired by young people actively seeking to be genuine disciples of the Risen Christ in today's church.

On an international level, the United Nations voted to repudiate the Doctrine of Discovery in 2012. Following such sentiment, many countries have taken seriously the Kyoto Protocol and more recently, the Paris Accord of 2015. Denmark and the Netherlands have emerged as European leaders in this effort.

The book *Care for Creation* suggests that this current global climate crisis should awaken us to respond to what our present lifestyle is doing to Earth's outdoor environment. (See Delio, Warner, and Wood, *Care For Creation: A Franciscan Spirituality of the Earth*, 2008)

In the Creation, God called all living things to care for Earth. God created them to share with God in the stewardship of the continuing Creation. Through God we are caught up in the flowing spirit of the WORD. Saint Francis worshipped God the harmony of the Creation. When we worship God outdoors in God's Holy Temple, we should feel surrounded by God's unconditional love, as Saint Francis did.

A Larger Context of Space and Time

The Music of Silence by Brother David Steindl-Rast (see above, Chapter 1) suggests another dimension of time. In our indoor colonial civilization, we are limited by clock and calendar time. Earth-time travels with the Creation in a larger context.

Brother David speaks to this larger time perspective in his presentation of the "Music of Silence".

It is time that fills itself while one is otherwise occupied. When one accepts gratitude as the basis for building and growing one's relationship with God, praying the Lord's prayer facilitates authentic worship, as one increasingly listens to the Spirit.

The Lord's Prayer begins with "Our Father". Jesus is calling us to pray together in community. As we listen intently to the inner voice of God, we are also listening to each other in the appropriate intimacy of a community praying together. Such listening causes us to slow down. Accordingly, we acquire the time we need to feel more of what is going on around us.

Our modern lifestyle is consumed by a perpetually compulsive, frantic pace of life, hoping to "save time". In contrast, slowing down gives us more time to explore the infinite possibilities that God has prepared for us to indulge in presently. God outdoors allows us to become aware of the splendor of God (Psalm 104). We can indulge in worship itself as stewardship, as we slow down to what I call "godspeed".

If we are to be disciples of Jesus, we need to adopt the lifestyle that allows us to become "gentle and humble of heart", in order to learn from Jesus, as we take on his yoke and follow him (Matthew 11:28-30). In his book *On God's Side*, Jim Wallis articulates such stewardship of the Jesus lifestyle that calls his followers to always seek to serve the common good. (See Wallis, *On God's Side: What Religion Forgets, and Politics Hasn't Learned About Serving the Common Good*, 2013)

Abraham's Covenant with God

The covenant enabled the descendants of Abraham to systematically accumulate the unique relationships they developed with God in the process of worshiping God. People in the oral tradition usually lived in intimate communities, committed to honoring the common good. They lived by the principle that it takes a village to raise children who looked after each other as they had been looked after.

Many had special occasions when they would pray together for days. Native Americans had the sweat lodge ceremonies. Jesus used Aramaic as the language of choice in most of his interactions with his audience, because it encouraged the intimacy of the village raising children, who would naturally care for each other.

The Rich Blessing of the Shutdown

The emergence of the coronavirus pandemic of 2020 has forced a global response, which has effectively shut down international travel and grounded over 90% of normal airline traffic. The truth of Earth's lifestyle in the pandemic has required us to adopt social distance and rely on virtual closeness. In the days of the Old Testament people were physically isolated by distance. They did not have airlines. They did not have the internet. They understood real time and increased its availability by slowing down.

In the village that raises the child, such a community sees continuous value in each child. In such a village, the common good is the element of greatest value. Thus, when they talked about "the people", they sought the truths related to celebrating the common good. This is what Jesus means when he says: "Worship the God of unconditional love and compassion in spirit and in truth". The Coronavirus shutdown has slowed us down to control its spread. The countries and communities that have slowed down and pursued the common good have been most effective in slowing its spread.

Sacred Silence

In the USA, the popular media seeks to fill every second of broadcast time with excessive chatter. Most of the chatter seeks to hastily control our behavior. Silence seems taboo! However, for personal control, we should use the "mute" button to avoid the mindless chatter.

The Sermon on the Mount spells it out in the Beatitudes. Those who follow Jesus and live by the spirit of the Father and have been blessed. Moreover, because they have been blessed by God through their communication with God in spirit, their commitment to the covenant makes them a spontaneous blessing to all who they encounter, making them "bless-ed"!

The Bible translations that replace "bless-ed" with "happy" miss the point. "Happy" is how I feel, when things go well. In contrast, we are always filled with the joy of the covenant, and we become "bless-ed and joyful"!

The Jesus Lifestyle is Inclusive

In the Sermon on the Mount Jesus is telling his Aramaic listeners that they are a blessing, to God, to each other and to the kingdom of heaven (Matthew 5: 3-20). Cynthia Bourgeault, in her book *Wisdom Jesus*, describes the spirit of the Beatitudes in the way Jesus may have shared them with his disciples. They became his followers. He says: You feel terrible most of the time, but you are a blessing to God, as you are. You are mournful at present, but you shall be comforted. You are meek, but you shall inherit the earth. You hunger and thirst for righteousness, and you shall be filled. You, who are merciful shall receive mercy. You, who have a pure heart will see God. You, who always make peace with your neighbor will be called the children of God. You, who are persecuted because you work for righteousness, will have great rewards in heaven. You, who are framed for my sake, or in the service of those around you, or you, who are set up to be punished for the misdeeds of others, rejoice and be exceedingly joyful, for great is your reward in heaven! You are the salt of the earth! You know how to enhance your saltiness! You are the light of the world: Let the world know you as you can be! Shine! They became his followers. (See: Cynthia Bourgeault, *Wisdom Jesus: Transforming Heart and Mind – A New Perspective on Christ and His Message*, 2008)

Such a Spirit of Discipleship is Offended by Much of the "American Way"

The "law and order" mentality of contemporary USA encourages the police in many communities to deny basic human dignity to non-Europeans. The spirit of the common good is not extended to the poor. As such, the government issued minimum wage establishes a specific dollar amount, generally less than a half an effective living wage. An honest minimum wage should be a living wage, tied to the cost of living in each community.

As mentioned above in Chapter 1, the European concept of democracy does not celebrate the "common good". From the book *Greenhouses of Hope* by Dori Grinenko Baker (editor) comes a relevant example of a person using her own personal challenge to be a blessing to others. Margaret Ann Crain sang in the adult choir as a teen and became president of her youth group at a United Methodist church in San Jose, California. As a young mother, having struggled with faith questions, she was invited to join the staff of her congregation with only on-the-job training and began to enroll in UNC training events. This led her all the way to a doctorate in religious education and a commitment to further ministry. Today she is an ordained deacon on the faculty of Garrett-Evangelical Theological Seminary, teaching Christian education. (See also: Wallis, *On God's Side: What Religion Forgets, and Politics Hasn't Learned About Serving the Common Good*, 2013, pp. 3-7)

In effect, applying herself to care for her village, she grew to uplift herself and the village. Her story is discussed to display another example of her work with young people seeking to follow the Jesus lifestyle out of their particular combination of opportunities (see Chapter 5).

Young People Are Extending Their Dreams to Excite a Global Appeal

On Monday 23 September 2019 a 16 year-old environmental activist, Greta Thunberg from Sweden, addressed the United Nations, accusing world leaders of inaction and half-measures in response to the current global climate crisis. Here are her remarks (as reported by NBC News on September 23, 2019, 2:07 PM PDT):

> My message is that we'll be watching you.
>
> This is all wrong. I shouldn't be up here. I should be back in school on the other side of the ocean. Yet, you all come to us young people for hope. How dare you!
>
> You have stolen my dreams and my childhood with your empty words and yet I'm one of the lucky ones. People are suffering. People are dying. Entire ecosystems are collapsing. We are in the beginning of a mass extinction and all you can talk about is money and fairytales of economic growth. How dare you!

For more than 30 years, the science has been crystal clear. How dare you continue to look away and come here saying you're doing enough when the politics and solutions needed are still nowhere in sight.

You say you hear us and that you understand the urgency, but no matter how sad and angry I am, I do not want to believe that. Because if you really understood the situation and still kept on failing to act then you would be evil and I refuse to believe.

The popular idea of cutting our emissions in half in 10 years only gives us a 50 percent chance of staying below 1.5 degrees and risk setting off irreversible chain reaction beyond human control.

Fifty percent may be acceptable to you, but those numbers do not include tipping points, most feedback loops, additional warming hidden by toxic air pollution or the aspects of equity and climate justice.

They also rely on my generation sucking hundreds of billions of tons of your CO2 out of the air with technologies that barely exist. So, a 50% risk is simply not acceptable to us, we who have to live with the consequences.

How dare you pretend that this can be solved with just business as usual and some technical solutions? **With today's emission levels, that remaining CO2 budget will be entirely gone within less than eight and a half years** (Author's emphasis).

There will not be any solutions or plans presented in line with these figures here today, because these numbers are too uncomfortable and you are still not mature enough to tell it like it is.

You are failing us, but the young people are starting to understand your betrayal. The eyes of all future generations are upon you and if you choose to fail us, I say: We will never forgive you.

We will not let you get away with this. Right here, right now is where we draw the line. The world is waking up and change is coming, whether you like it or not.

At first, the United Nations took no official action. However, *Time Magazine* awarded Greta Thunberg "Person of The Year" of 2019. She is the youngest person and the first teen ever to earn this Time Magazine award.

The World Council of Churches Proposed a Resolution at the United Nations in 2012 to Repudiate the Doctrine of Discovery

The resolution was adopted almost unanimously. No country opposed it. However, a few countries abstained, notably the USA, Canada and Australia. Many Christian denominations have applauded the repudiation. The World Council of Churches sought to celebrate the spirit of the Jesus lifestyle. Jesus taught his disciples the following:

"Come to me all you that are weary and are carrying heavy burdens, and I will give you rest. Take my yoke upon you and learn from me; for I am gentle and humble in heart, and you will find rest in your soul. For my yoke is easy and my burden is light" (Matthew 11:25-30).

"God is spirit and those, who worship him must worship in spirit and truth" (John 4:24, read John 4:7-42 for the full story).

"All authority in Heaven and on Earth has been given to me. Go, therefore and make disciples of all nations, baptizing them in the name of the Father and of the Son and of the Holy Spirit, and teaching them to obey everything that I have commanded of you. And remember, I am with you always, to the end of the age" (Matthew 28:18-20).

"Love one another as I have loved You. Greater love has no one than this to lay down one's life for one's friend. You are my friends if you do what I command you. I do not call you servant any longer, because the servant does not know what the master is doing; but I have called you friends, because I have made known to you everything I have heard from my Father. You did not choose me, but I have chosen you. And I appoint you to go and bear fruit, fruit that will last, so that the Father will give you whatever you ask him in my name. I am giving you these commandments so that you may love one another as I have loved you" (John 13:31-35, 14:25-27).

"First you love the Lord, your God with all your heart, with all your soul and with all your mind and with all your strength. Also, you should love your neighbor as yourself" (Matthew 22:37-40).

Consider a possible Creed adopted by a disciple of Jesus based on the Jesus lifestyle. The God of splendor showers us all with unconditional love and is full of compassion. Jesus calls us to share such love and compassion with everyone we meet, serving each other in love and kindness. Accordingly, I suggest the following Creed to replace the one handed down by Emperor Constantine, son of Caesar:

> I believe God is Spirit and Jesus called his disciples to worship God in spirit and in truth and to adopt the Jesus lifestyle.

> I believe Jesus called us to worship God outdoors in God's Holy Temple.

> I believe that in God's Holy Temple we feel surrounded by the unconditional love and compassion of God and can relate more naturally to the image of God in which we are all created.

> I believe all authority has been given to Jesus, the Risen Christ to send his disciples to make disciples of all nations, baptizing them in the name of the Father and of the Son and of the Holy Spirit, teaching them to obey and observe everything

that Jesus has commanded us and to remember that Jesus is with us to the end of the age.

I believe that Jesus has called us all to love one another as Jesus has loved us all. He calls us friend, so that, as we adopt his lifestyle, whatever we ask in the name of Jesus would be granted.

I believe that by adopting and sharing God's unconditional love and compassion with our neighbors and praying the Lord's Prayer, I would grow in my strength to worship God, listen to God's will in my life and come to know God better.

I believe Jesus has given us all the gift of forgiveness to share freely with our neighbor, so that we would all carry his yoke with him, together.

I believe Jesus has taught us that kindness is contagious!

The relevance of the voice of Greta Thunberg is critical to the COVID-19 pandemic. The General Secretary of the United Nations, Sec. Antonio Guterres, addresses the critical services and concerns of the United Nations in the pandemic, in Chapter 5 - The Harmony of Earth's Lifestyle is worth special consideration. He includes the appeal of Greta in his address.

In a New York Times report: "This is the World Being Left to Us by Adults" by Greta Thunberg, Adriana Calderon, Farzana Faruk Jhumu and Eric Njuguna. The report revealed that some of the world's leading scientists confirmed that the extreme weather conditions being experienced were irreversible. A new UNICEF release identified about 850 million children, one-third of the current world population of children, were being exposed to 4 or more climate and environmental hazards and were already living in irreversible poverty and starvation. The United Nations Secretary General was making this his top priority.

Chapter 4

The Doctrine of Discovery Sent European Christians on a Mission to Convert or Eradicate Non-Europeans as Enemies of God

The primary purpose of this mission was to promote the perpetual slavery of all non-Europeans. It entrusted the religion of European Christianity to evangelize the European church in this new religion in 1452.

In 2012, The United Nations voted to repudiate the Doctrine of Discovery. It was the culmination of a campaign undertaken by the World Council of Churches over several years. It began not long after a World Council Conference, which I attended as a freshman at the University of Michigan. The

Conference at Ohio University in Athens, Ohio, December 1961 was entitled: "For the Life of the World".

In addition, the core legal codes and governance in the colonial empires was based on this Doctrine. European Christianity has grown out of the religion of Emperor Constantine, as articulated at the Council of Nicaea in 325, AD. Thus, in his action to make his Christianity a department of the Roman Empire, he reduced the mission of Jesus to a following of Roman pagan rituals. Henceforth, European Christianity would imagine Jesus and almost all people of the Old Testament as European.

Accordingly, indigenous peoples living under the rule of European colonies today are dispossessed former slaves. Many still occupy a part of their God-given ancestral lands, which they had occupied for tens of thousands of years prior to the first appearance of Europeans. Under such governance, the invading Europeans systematically ignored the humanity of the indigenous people and treated them as foreigners on their God-given land.

More than half of the USA population is currently poverty-stricken, including most of the indigenous North Americans. These, as well as, African, Asian and others who came to work these lands, were treated like imported slaves.

The Doctrine of Discovery Used Heresy Against Non-Europeans to Engineer a Global Racism Pandemic

When the USA calls itself "America", it seeks to permanently displace the indigenous people of the Americas. The Spanish-American war formalized that intention. Such development has created a concentration of chronic poverty here in the Americas. These destitute people of Central and South America cannot acquire legal entry into the USA. Thus, they have become "illegal aliens", making them the most underpaid laborers in the USA.

The Most Vulnerable Americans Living in the USA Are Indigenous

Rev. Marguerite Watson, an Episcopal priest, of European descent, on the Cheyenne River Reservation was from Berkeley, California and, in a report published by Vinnie Rotondaro in 2015, she had been serving the Cheyenne River for four years. She remained acutely aware of the pain and suffering in the 10 congregations she served on the reservation, which is roughly the size of the state of Connecticut.

Much of her time was spent conducting funerals. Many were suicides committed by children as young as 12-years old. Residents regularly came to her door asking for help, sometimes for food, sometimes for money, sometimes because they saw something, or felt something, and needed spiritual comfort. She handled conflicts common to the inner city: guns, violence and gang activity, too. But death was most prevalent. Watson explained that her priestly duties include a lot of liturgy. "Book work and paperwork hold me accountable to the diocese. ... Prayers from the heart — I was brought up saying prayers from a book, so I really tried to learn to pray from the heart, and still be theologically cognizant. ... I do a lot of anointing and healing prayer. ... I do some pastoral counseling. ... I've been asked to clean a house of spooks or ghosts or spirits".

"The suicide rate is off the map", Watson said. Each year, between five and six people under the age of 25 take their life. For her part, Hollow Horn, one of her faithful congregants, said she has attended "about 29" suicide funerals, young and old, in his lifetime. Watson, who lives in Eagle Butte with her husband, Joel, also an Episcopal priest, said she has averaged 55 burials a year since coming to Cheyenne River. This is her fourth year. "There are two types of suicide on this reservation", she said. "Slow and fast. Drinking and drugs and diet. Diabetes is so prevalent around here". She added, "I would say about 70 percent of the people I bury are under the age of 50. Those under the age of 30 are accidents, drunk driving, or suicide. And those between the age of 30 and 50 are drugs and alcohol. At least two a year freeze to death". Watson said that 20 percent of the funerals she presided over the last year were for infants or stillborn children. "Some families I see two and three times a year to bury a family member", she said.[1]

Rev. Watson introduced Karen Ducheneaux, the daughter of Candace Ducheneaux, who keeps a detailed account of the poverty that exists in Cheyenne River. Over the past few years, she helped perform research for a charitably funded study called "Cheyenne River Voices" that created a "baseline data source" for the reservation, not unlike the U.S. Census. However, her research revealed a more accurate population count, which gave a lower per capita income and a more realistic picture of the poverty on the reservation. "In a lot of ways our data differs" from that of the U.S. Census, Ducheneaux said. The reservation population that the study tallied, for instance, was about 25 percent higher than that of the census — 10,564 versus 8,470. Similarly, "when we calculated income, it came out much, much, much lower, about half of what the United States identifies", Ducheneaux said.

---

1. See: "Doctrine of Discovery: A Scandal in Plain Sight", by Vinnie Rotondaro, *The Trail of History*, National Catholic Reporter, September 5, 2015.

According to the "Cheyenne River Voices" report, the median annual income for reservation families is $18,156. Meanwhile, annual family expenses are listed at a median of $14,055. "That means you only have $4,000 of disposable income [a year] to save or to take your kids to a doctor's appointment", Ducheneaux said. "We're just talking about utilities, and monthly bills, like car payments, credit card payments ... that's $300 a month for our families to do all their business. On top of it all, the infrastructure in Cheyenne River is old and failing. Our water system put a moratorium on building", Ducheneaux said. "You cannot build a new house; you cannot put a house where a water pit does not already exist. There are no empty houses. There are no houses sitting around for rent". In Cheyenne River, about 75 percent of the tribe is currently living in poverty or hovering just above it, Ducheneaux estimates. "Even people with jobs", she said, "if something happens and they miss one paycheck, it just collapses". (See: Vinnie Rotondaro, "Doctrine of Discovery: A Scandal in Plain Sight", *The Trail of History*, National Catholic Reporter, September 5, 2015)

The Trail of History is the sixth part of a six-part series on the Doctrine of Discovery written by Vinnie Rotondaro. It details the impact of the Doctrine on colonial Christianity in the new world. Such information and relevant impressions are readily accessible to those willing to listen. Accordingly, we should embark on genuine listening, with generous self-forgiving.

The community of Cheyenne River has a story to share: "There was nothing we could do about it", Ducheneaux said. "My father was a lead negotiator for the tribe, and when he went into those talks, he began the negotiations on a somber note. He said, 'This is not a happy occasion. We are here to participate in the gutting of our reservation.'" Her story illustrates the injustice her people live with, but more generally, the heartache they endure. This history of imperialism drives the suffering and suicide that exists in Indian country today. But from deep within that history, "the Catholic faith and the Christian religion is exalted and everywhere increased and spread, that the health of souls be cared for and that barbarous nations be overthrown and brought to the faith itself". Instead of being encountered like human beings, native people were said to have been "discovered", like some new species of animal.

The heresy code enforcement administration had inflicted greater persecution on the followers of the Jesus lifestyle than any other single group. They were not familiar with the Roman pagan rituals implied by the Council of Nicaea. Christian Heresy hunters, as the Inquisitor Francesco Pena stated in 1578, announced: "We must remember that the main purpose of the trial and execution is not to save the soul of the accused but to achieve the public good and put fear into others". The Inquisition took countless human lives in Europe and around the world as it followed in the wake of missionaries. And along with the tyranny of the Inquisition, churchmen also brought religious justification for the practice of slavery. The un-submissive spirit of the Middle Ages only seemed to exacerbate the Church's demand for unquestioning obedience. The Church's understanding of God was to be the only understanding. There was to be no discussion or debate. As the Inquisitor Bernard Gui said, the layman must not argue with the unbeliever, but "thrust his sword into the man's belly as far as it will go". In a time of burgeoning ideas about spirituality, the Church insisted that it was the only avenue through which one was permitted to learn of God. Pope Innocent III declared "that anyone who attempted to construe a personal view of God which conflicted with Church dogma must be burned without pity".[2]

Historical Impacts

Deep psychological wounds hamper life in Cheyenne River today. European traders had been visiting the land and had already inflicted the European male slave master disease on the indigenous natives. The survivors were sometimes attacked by the new arrivals from Europe, or otherwise had their settlements plundered. Marcella Le Beau, a Lakota tribal elder living in Eagle Butte, tells her own family history to explain this reality, recalling her great-grandfather, Joseph Four Bear, who signed the Treaty of Fort Laramie of 1868, and how the process of being forced onto a reservation demoralized her ancestors.

Following a period of war between the U.S. and Great Plains tribes over routes to gold fields in Montana (the routes crossed tribal land), the Fort Laramie Treaty established the Great Sioux Reservation, stretching across half of South Dakota and a small part of modern-day Nebraska. It guaranteed Lakota proprietorship of the Black Hills, which they hold sacred, as well as hunting rights in South Dakota, Wyoming and Montana. But some viewed the treaty negatively. Its provisions were dense and complicated; the lead-up to its signing was tense and filled with violence. Furthermore, a semi-nomadic people were now geographically contained. Le Beau believes that her great-grandfather signed the treaty "under duress". Soon after its signing, key provisions were broken. Such was the case when gold was discovered in the Black Hills, and prospectors crossed onto reservation land, and war ensued.

In 1877, the U.S. took the Black Hills, which included Mount Rushmore. Into the mountain's granite, huge sculptures of four U.S. presidents would be carved, creating a memorial that opened in 1941. In 1889, more land was lost when Congress voted to partition the Great Sioux Reservation into five smaller reservations. Then, in December 1890, with tension building and the Ghost Dance phenomenon — a brand of mysticism that foresaw a new age of power for American Indians — unnerving white America, the revered Lakota warrior Sitting Bull was killed by tribal police. Responding to news of his death, The *Aberdeen Saturday Pioneer* wrote: "The Whites, by law of conquest, by justice of civilization, are masters of the American continent, and the best safety of the frontier settlements will be secured by the total annihilation of the few remaining Indians". The author of the story, L. Frank Baum, later became famous, penning *The Wonderful Wizard of Oz*. Two weeks after Sitting Bull's death, the Lakota were dealt a crushing blow when U.S. forces massacred Native American men, women and children at Wounded Knee River on the Pine Ridge reservation in South Dakota. "I did not know then how much was ended", Lakota holy man Black Elk later wrote. "When I look back now from this high hill of my old age, I can still see the butchered women and children lying heaped and scattered all along the crooked gulch as plain as when I saw them with eyes still young. And I can see that something else died there in the bloody mud and was buried in the blizzard. A people's dream died there. It was a beautiful dream". (See: Vinnie Rotondaro, "Doctrine of Discovery: A Scandal in Plain Sight", *The Trail of History,* National Catholic Reporter, September 5, 2015)

The basic economies of the colonies were raped to build up the economies of Europe. The USA, Canada and other former colonies where Europeans have settled in significant numbers (Australia, New Zealand) became European countries. The colonies with non-European majorities are some of the most poverty-stricken countries in the world today.

Although the Doctrine of Discovery was repudiated by the World Council of Churches at the United Nations in 2012, the Nicene Creed is still being recited in churches today. In effect, European Christianity continues to dominate the global Christian practice in violation of the scriptures it claims to follow.

Chapter 5
The Harmony of Earth's Lifestyle

Everything about the Creation is a 'story' because no person was there to record the event. Throughout the world, indigenous people have passed on the stories taught by their respective ancestors. Humans have lived on Earth for about one million years. Until some 5,000 years ago almost all the world's population spoke unwritten languages. Most of these societies lived in conscious harmony with Earth's lifestyle. Jared Diamond, in his book *The World until Yesterday*, describes the lifestyles and customs of people in traditional societies throughout the world. He describes people, who he has studied in New Guinea and parts of South America, living as most of the world lived 5,000 years ago. (See: Diamond, Jared, *The World until Yesterday: What can we learn from Traditional Societies?*, 2012.)

Their sense of interdependence is still the most humane approach to communities seeking to live in harmony in today's societies. Chapter 1 introduced us to the effect of people in traditional society, who lived in harmony with Earth's lifestyle. Their lifestyle focused on striving for "the common good".

The colonial era enforced a different European approach. It was built on a lifestyle that would depend on the perpetual slavery of non-Europeans. The Doctrine of Discovery, outlined in the Introduction, was the beginning of the colonial era of European Christianity, which was spread throughout the world, as shown in the Appendix.

Chapters 1 to 3 used the scriptures to outline the Jesus lifestyle to which he introduced his disciples and instructed them to teach "to all nations". The alternative creed in Chapter 3 seeks to better represent the Jesus lifestyle, which he calls us to follow in his name.

Jesus Called His Disciples to Share His Yoke in Their Daily Lives

Living with the yoke Jesus gave his disciples requires us to care for each other's well-being and protect "the common good". It is in essence the stewardship that "takes a village to raise a child". A group of mothers generally led traditional societies. They raised the male and female children together, encouraging them to look after each other. This is still common among many indigenous communities throughout the world and is fully sustainable.

Earth's lifestyle flows in harmony with the spirit that worships God in God's Holy Temple. The European indoor lifestyle does not easily appreciate Earth's lifestyle. Many of the people of the oral tradition lived like the plants and animals, in harmony with Earth's lifestyle. Their resulting stewardship of Earth's environment allowed them to use time in ways very different from the modern time perspective, which is limited to clock and calendar time.

To appreciate the limits of our modern time perspective, the recent history of Nevado del Ruiz in Colombia illustrates such time limits. In 1845 the mountain volcano erupted at night some 70 km from the village of Armero. The flow of lava from the volcano wiped out the village of about 5,000, killing almost all its inhabitants. In time, people forgot about the 1845 disaster and resettled on the lava flow of the previous volcano. In 1984, when Nevado del Ruiz began to show signs of an impending eruption, a young scientist, Marta Calveche, who had been studying the 1845 eruption went to the mayor of the town that Armero had become, to explain the way volcanoes tell us that they are about to erupt. He made fun of her inability to give the exact date and time of the eruption. It erupted on a rainy night and the lava flowed through the town, trapping and killing over 20,000, including people, who struggled and eventually died as they tried to walk out of acres of hot lava that flowed for weeks. (See Romain, *Observing*

Earth's Lifestyle, Considering the Value of Earth Stewardship in Environmental Protection, pp. 56-57, 2017)

In the context of God and the scriptures, there are other time concepts to be grasped. In the *Music of Silence*, written by Br. David Steindl-Rast, he talks of "Chronos" and "Kairos". Earth harmony allows indigenous people to slow down and allow normal earth-time to last longer for the task at hand.

Pierre Teilhard de Chardin incorporated the Geological records of fourteen billion years ago into his St. Ignatius studies of the 15th century. Accordingly, he presented Ignatian spirituality in the context of modern science. De Chardin was a geologist who believed that the St. Ignatius exercises were accurate, scientific expressions of God's Creation. See the following study, which outlines specific themes contained in de Chardin's extensive studies. Pierre Teilhard de Chardin was a geologist, paleontologist, French philosopher, who studied extensively in China. As a Jesuit scholar, he was exploring his work in the context of Ignatian Spirituality. He was born in France in 1881 and died in New York City in April 1955. (See Savary, *In the Spirit of Pierre Teilhard de Chardin*, 2011)

Post-Colonial Christianity Leads Us Away from The Jesus Lifestyle

As Howard Thurman points out in his book *Jesus and the Disinherited*, Jesus is the subject, not the object of his discourse. Jesus came to lead his people back to their authentic and inherited culture, civilization and religion. Jesus was an unashamed Jew, seeking to reestablish the covenant that God had made with his oldest ancestor, Abraham (see Chapter 3). His thesis is that non-Europeans need to rise above the intimidation of the Christianity that we have inherited, in order to become true disciples of Jesus.

This is what Jesus, himself, was doing when he called his disciples to follow him. They were the disinherited children of Israel in their own land, occupied by the Roman Empire.

Howard Thurman suggests that Jesus, himself was somewhat disinherited in his own village. Thurman uses how Jesus taught and led his disciples to appeal to African Americans and other former slaves in the USA and the other colonies to learn from the ways Jesus demonstrated in his lifestyle to build community and serve God. (See Thurman, *Jesus and the Disinherited*, 1976)

In their exile from the covenant during the time of Jesus, the Jews had come to see themselves as God's exclusive chosen.

In truth, everyone is created in the image of God. As such we are all God's chosen people (Genesis 1: 20-28). Both Jesus and John the Baptist emphasized to their respective disciples that God shared unconditional love and compassion with everyone. This was further clarified to the disciples by Jesus in teaching them to pray the Lord's Prayer (Luke 11:1-13).

God wants all the disciples of Jesus to follow him through the eye of the needle, discussed in Chapter 2. Jesus commanded this of his faithful following, so that whatever they asked in his name would be granted. He called them to: "Love one another as I have loved You. Greater love has no one than this to lay down one's life for one's friend. You are my friends if you do what I command you. I did not call you servant, because the servant does not know what the master is doing; but I have called you friends, because I have made known to you everything I have heard from my Father. You did not choose me, but I have chosen you. And I appoint you to go and bear fruit, fruit that will last, so that the Father will give you whatever you ask him in my name. I am giving you these commandments so that you may love one another" (John 13: 31-35).

The Coronavirus Pandemic Offers an Opportunity to Love One Another as Jesus Loves Each of Us

Many non-European victims of perpetual slavery have found their way directly to Jesus. Bryan Stevenson discusses the concept of Howard Thurman's thesis on Jesus, as the disinherited Jew. In Stevenson's book *Just Mercy*, he provides another powerful testimony of one, who uncovered a legal series of systems in the USA designed to systematically multiply and intensify the persecution of non-European citizens. Bryan Stevenson is a Defense Attorney, who has committed himself to defending African Americans on death row in prisons across the country, who have been accused of murders they did not commit. During his investigations, he became aware of other victims whose plight has been created by a normal acceptable range of incredible legal police abuses. (See Stevenson, *Just Mercy*, 2014)

Basic democracy suggests that justice would lead to active support for the common good of its citizens. According to the Jesus lifestyle Archbishop Tutu used his Ubuntu theology to promote the reconciliation that brought healing to South Africa. The principles of truth and reconciliation eventually enabled the common good to regain the principles of their indigenous oral tradition. Bryan Stevenson's pursuit of "just mercy" reveals what can emerge from the genuine appeal to the common good for fellow citizens.

The US Interpretation of "The American Way" is Built on Consuming Contradictions

The status of its citizenry is unequal. The individual rights of Europeans are designed to own and exploit the humanity of all non-European citizens. The self-worship of its European male leadership is further designed to enslave all European females as preferred property and second-class citizens. Such contradictory principles require continuous enforcement, because it is inherently unnatural for all living beings.

Furthermore, the impact of "the American way" on the other people of the Americas, results in the non-Europeans among them being treated worse than Europeans in the USA. In other words, European Christianity has so corrupted the understanding of God and Jesus in the minds and hearts of European colonial subjects that most colonial young people today are inclined to feel alienated from God.

The Value of Supporting the Common Good

The communities throughout the world that have reduced the coronavirus spread most effectively have focused on serving the common good. South Korea and Australia are two of many good examples observed in 2021. In Chapter 5 the South Korean community's focus on the common good is discussed in detail.

The Australian government openly discussed and implemented its effort to reduce the coronavirus spread as it hosted the 2022 Australian Open Tennis Tournament, a major global annual sporting event. Other exemplary countries include Vietnam and Thailand. They have effectively controlled the spread of the COVID-19 pandemic.

The increasing deaths among young people in the USA was particularly alarming, especially as then President Trump refused to wear masks and contracted the virus himself weeks before the election. The infection spread rapidly through his staff and their families. Yet, he tried to give the impression that he had recovered sufficiently to get back to business as usual after a few days.

Defeating the Spread of the Coronavirus Requires Virtual Intimacy

We have been forced to live with virtual intimacy. In such intimacy, Jesus offers to share his yoke, by following his two commandments: Matthew 22:37-40. He tells us that he is "gentle and humble in heart and you will find rest in your souls. For my yoke is easy and my burden is light". Such a humble posture invited his followers to a deeper humility. When we pursue such connections with gratitude and kindness, we share good tidings as Jesus calls us to do, carrying his yoke. His last words to his disciples before ascending into heaven, (Matthew 28: 18-20): "All authority in Heaven and on Earth has been given to me. Go, therefore, and make disciples of all nations, baptizing them in the name of the Father and of the Son and of the Holy Spirit and teaching them to obey everything that I have commanded you. And remember, I am with you always, to the end of the age." (From: *The Green Bible*. New Revised Standard Version Bible, Division of Christian Education of the National Council of Churches of Christ in the United States of America. , 1989)

Eventually, the voters in the Presidential Election overwhelmingly elected Joe Biden to be the next President, over Donald Trump. As suggested earlier, a growing movement of young people in many congregations was rising up to claim their commitment to carry the yoke with Jesus. The young people voting in the election heavily supported the Biden campaign. As such, President-elect Joe Biden received 51% of the votes – over 81,200,000, compared with 47% of the votes – over 74,200,000 to President Trump.

New York Was Hardest Hit by the Coronavirus

On 7 April news carried a story on two Emergency Medical Transport, (EMT) drivers in New York City. They welcomed the opportunity to help in the city's disaster. However, their biggest fear was the possibility that they may contaminate their own families. Each earned $37,000/year, a poverty wage for a family in New York City. In normal peace time, both had other jobs to supplement their income. In this crisis there was no time for other jobs!

This painful irony is accentuated in the USA, where the poor in communities of great wealth become virtually invisible on several levels. Moreover, the economy is expressed specifically to cover up the fact that it takes thousands of poor families to make up the taxes that the rich do not pay to run the country financially.

Dori Grinenko Baker, editor of *Greenhouses of Hope,* begins her book with a description of her project and why she started writing it. It is a description of what she appreciates about getting to know God in God's Holy Temple. Despite the news of churches losing attendance and closing, she saw "green shoots emerging". She saw young people in congregations looking for and pursuing new paths they were discovering. Some were starting college in one career path and discovering that other side issues with more excitement appealed to them. In her words, she explained: "I name these churches 'Greenhouses of Hope'. A Greenhouse of Hope is a Christian congregation, freeing itself to experiment with both newly imagined and time-honored ways of following the path of Jesus. Its members respond to God's love through practices that genuinely embrace the gifts of youth and young adults. Out of these greenhouses emerge young leaders who want to change the world". (See: Baker, editor, *Greenhouses of Hope*, p. 2, 2010)

With this definition in mind, she has been traveling the country, talking with church leaders with similar interests and comparable projects. In the process, she distilled a unique research project in ethnography. In October 2008 a group gathered to dream about churches they knew and churches they did not yet know that would support young people in vocational discovery. The following professors at denominational seminaries included: Fred Edie, Katherine Turpin, Joyce Mercer, Margaret Ann Crain and Jeffery Tribble. They were joined by Sinai Chung, a recent doctoral graduate and Melissa

Wiginton, vice president of ministry programs and planning for The Fund for Theological Education (FTE). The stories of a few of these experts will be used later in this chapter to highlight young leaders changing the world.

Down the Road from Where I Live

Occasionally, your most dramatic life-changing event pops up in your neighborhood. Dori Grinenko Baker discovered the Greenhouse of Hope "down the road from where I live in Virginia". She was looking for a project that she could use to engage young people seeking to change their world. These greenhouses had been abandoned for years and were becoming a source of new innovative projects for local young people to revive through their own experiments. These are her own comments:

> Here is the oasis I saw: red Swiss chard, lemon trees, arugula, sweet aromatic basil, sage and bananas, all thriving in pots and raised beds; green peppers and tomatoes ripening in the warm air; a pond nurturing tiny bluegill, whose waste will feed the neighboring spinach. Marky, a special needs student from a nearby high school showed me around, while Derek, a thirty-seven-year-old

survivor of spina bifida, watered a green tangling cucumber vine heavy-laden with fruit that would be picked, sold and eaten on the same day. As I emerged from one greenhouse, I found a dozen school children making fragrant bouquets of rose, sage and basil to take home at the end of their field trip. Outside another greenhouse, I met a recent college graduate who had just completed an internship at the garden. Enthused about how much fun he'd had teaching children where food came from, that fresh food combats obesity and those fresh veggies straight from the garden "actually taste good". He had changed his major to an emphasis on agricultural education.

A sign at another greenhouse celebrated the fact that 95% of the produce raised by the parishioners from St. John's Episcopal Church had gone to feed the hungry through local food banks. In the final greenhouse, I was knocked off my feet by the fragrance of one particular rose – called a lavande – the ancestor of an ancient root distinctive among today's commercially grown roses, because you can actually smell it. Found during renovation, the lavande rose was lovingly tended back to flourishing.

The Gratitude of Humility

The project, Greenhouses of Hope speaks to the almost infinite ways revealed to us, when we reach out to provide young people with meaningful challenges, when developing their relationship with God. It is particularly powerful, when they are encouraged to discuss and compare the different moments in which they hear God speaking to them. Repeatedly, young people in each group discussed stronger challenges to increase their faith in God that made them feel uncomfortable. For them it expressed the gratitude of humility, which one experiences, while carrying the yoke with Jesus. It strengthens one's discipleship commitment.

Cultivating an Ethnographic Disposition

In order to retain a tangible basis for comparison among the different programs four core "CARE" practices were considered:

C – Create hospitable space to explore Christian vocation.

A – Ask self-awakening questions.

R – Reflect theologically on self and community; and

E – Explore, enact, and establish ministry opportunities.

These core practices were further described on pages 30-31 of her book. (See Baker, editor, *Greenhouses of Hope*, 2010)

Margaret Ann Crain described her program "Staying Awake" at First United Methodist Church (FUMC) in Evanston, Illinois. She was meeting Emily for the first time, a college senior grappling with her choices for the future. Yet, she felt connected to her youth group and was convinced that whatever choices she made would be guided by her relationship with God and the group community. Her Christian life **was** her daily life. She had brought back from a summer project with children in Appalachia impressions to compare with those of the children in the city of Evanston. On another mission trip she had helped build schools in Ghana.

These reflections had pushed Emily to change her major to apply the challenges from her summer experiences. Her accepted lifestyle would continue to leave her open to endless exploration.

"God is bringing something out of me!" she deduced, seeing service as a part of her life, like eating! She is the oldest of three children of color adopted by white parents. She is black and white of Puerto Rican heritage. Her brother has mental illness that has forced him to be placed away from home. She deals with these irregularities by writing songs, which she sings, as she seeks to capture the "God Moments" that pop up as answers to her prayers.

Margaret Ann Crain was supported by Rev. Dean Francis, who began to take Sunday services outside on the lawn overlooking Lake Michigan to affirm to the young people their potential leadership. She was particularly impressed that Emily looked forward to confronting the "things that kind of made you uncomfortable". The young people were more ethnically mixed and found that pedestrians would stop and join the service. Sundays on the lawn attracted joggers and dog walkers.

The congregation was changing. What had been a large white upper middle-class gathering had been transformed into a much smaller, but definitely more lively, younger family of 75-80% white, 15% African American, accompanied by a small Asian American attendance.

The Korean American Church "Mozying"

Sinai Chung, a youth program leader from Korea, joined the Greenhouses of Hope pilgrimage with a very different set of challenges. She had to quickly learn a great deal about the Korean church in the USA "on the run". The Korean congregations adopted an extended family system of support to help the young people overcome the anxiety created by living in the aggressively segregated society of the USA.

She arrived and found herself running after a group of high-energy teens and had to make sense of their program literally "on the run". All the children lived like brothers and sisters. Their parents were every child's parents (mothers and fathers). Grandparents joined into this large extended family, as the village raising its children together!

The Practice of Inclusion

Living in the intensely segregated society of the USA carried an immense burden that left each of the children feeling isolated at school. They looked different from "American children" and were made to feel unwelcome, unwanted and were subjected to much bullying. Thus, when they arrived in church the older children made it their immediate responsibility to seek out and connect with whoever seemed isolated. Each child was adopted in his, (or her) particular gathering. The goal was to make that person feel welcome and fully accepted in church.

This practice of inclusion became critical in another setting, when many would go back to Korea for part of their summer vacation. They would be isolated and alienated by the folks in Korea, who regarded them with some disdain, as the "American kids". However, the physical torment of segregation and bullying that they experienced in US schools was missing back in Korea.

The Practice of Passionate Prayer

Group prayer is common in many Korean American congregations. It would grow naturally out of the regular church service. However, unlike European church services, group prayer could last for hours, with loud, passionate singing, chanting, weeping by individuals in the group. It was all incorporated into the singing medley of praise, gratitude, mourning, petitions, reaching into individual, personal issues.

Mozying is a modelling technique that takes on a style reflecting the culture and structure of the group. Thus, as the older children model inclusion, the younger children learn to be inclusive because Jesus was inclusive.

Living Together

Dori Grinenko Baker engaged Katherine Turpin in a radical welcome approach to observing a Christian congregation actively practicing its Christianity through an interfaith perspective. The First Congregational Church of Berkeley (FCCB) was led by the compulsion of Shelly Dieterle, who as a young seminarian on the day after the 9/11 disaster decided to visit a nearby mosque, which was advertising a worship service. She talked a few friends into accompanying her and they were welcomed into the Farsi language worship service. Since then, Shelly Dieterle has taken interested FCCB members to celebrate Ramadan, with fasting at the mosque.

This experience has motivated other students to get to know the faiths of their friends, who have other faiths. Many of her friends admitted: "just getting to know others helps me to know myself better". They were somewhat inadvertently creating a covenant community (see the Chapter 1 discussion on praying the Lord's Prayer).

Similarly, exploring the faith of others elevated the understanding of their own faith. The diversity of young people living on college campuses in the USA makes these campuses some of the most religiously diverse communities in the USA.

Shelly Dieterle noticed that the students were hungry for the stories that were coming out of their exposure to the mosque to celebrate Ramadan, as well as the visits of the Muslims who attended FCCB activities. It reflected the reality that visiting someone's home allowed the hosts to be more comfortable revealing their vulnerabilities, the source of deeper friendship. In the process, they were engaging the CARE principles of the Greenhouses of Hope vocational pilgrimage (see above).

Many years later, in November 2009, the relationship with the Muslim community blossomed, when the killing of soldiers at Fort Hood in Texas was revealed on TV. That Sunday a Jazz Ensemble was providing the music for the service. The first speaker was Sam, a bartender in his mid-twenties who introduced himself as a secular college student, who grew up in a Southern Baptist tradition and moved to California to hike mountains, deserts and the coast. His voice began to break, and his partner lent her support. He continued to describe how FCCB had been the community that allowed him unusual growth. The anticipation of hugs at coffee hour got him out of bed on Sunday mornings.

As the service ended, a minister invited anyone who wanted to share Holy Communion. A small group gathered at the front. Both joy and concern flowed among a vast age range from twenties to nineties. A young woman wept as she prayed for the families of the Muslim perpetrators of the killings at Fort Hood.

Converging Streams

Fred P. Edie was a 19-Year-old college sophomore returning home for the summer break, with no particular plans, expecting to revive his self-employed lawn-care service in the neighborhood and expanding his guitar singing and song writing hobby. His church was Isle of Hope United Methodist Church (IOHUMC). Isle of Hope is a small island, about six miles around its circumference road. Everyone knew everyone. And that village raised him.

First, the church youth group needed someone to drive the aged school bus, which took kids on summer trips. He had to learn to drive the bus and obtain an appropriate driver's license. The first trip was to do white-water rafting on Ocoee River in the Appalachian foothills. A parent was driving a second, newer bus. Fred was leading, because he knew the way.

At one point he noticed that the other bus was not in his rear-view mirror. He pulled over to wait for them to catch up. Then two emergency vehicles with flashing lights raced by going in the opposite direction. He turned the bus around and followed them, to find that the other bus had been crashed and several children had been injured. Four children had to be taken back home. The others had minor injuries and were able to crowd into his bus and continue the trip.

Through the disaster, the children supported each other. They were very cooperative. At first, they gathered to pray, but soon they were ready to continue the trip, once the injured had been taken care of. The experience bonded them for the summer. During that first trip, he experienced something new: "Though our faith was immature, we rightly sensed that God was in the mix here. God had seen us through a harrowing experience. God had given us one another to love through thick and thin. We did so abundantly, taking nothing for granted".

Up to that summer he had never even vaguely considered a career in ministry. That trip changed his life. Three years later he was on his way to seminary. He is writing this article 30 years later as an ordained clergy person, teaching at a denominational seminary.

The Common Impact of Praying Together

Each of the above Greenhouses of Hope celebrate young people who pray together, for each other, fully believing that God is listening. They talk freely about their experiences with God when they compare their lives at home with those who they meet and work with on mission trips. They expect to feel uncomfortable when confronted by the misfortune of others. They pray to God to show them how better to serve.

In this way, God becomes our living companion. Genuine worship becomes a natural continuing part of their daily lives when we *pray* the Lord's Prayer as Jesus taught us in Luke 11: 1-4. It is a special privilege to occasionally pray together as a group outdoors in God's Holy Temple, as Jesus and his disciples did most of the time.

Chapter 6
Rendering Unto Caesar What is God's

Emperor Constantine rendered unto Caesar what was God's (Mark 12: 15-17; Luke 20: 20-26; Matthew 22: 15-22) at the Council of Nicaea. Emperor Constantine made the Church of Rome a department of the Roman Empire. He then created his own heresy code as an enforcement order designed to punish and root out the non-believers in his new Christianity. The Holy Catholic and Apostolic Church enforced the heresy code based on their familiar Roman pagan ritual, which began the fundamental heresy (see Introduction). The Desert Fathers and Mothers escaped to the deserts of Egypt and the Middle East, giving them the freedom to practice and preserve the customs of their genuine and faithful discipleship, removed from the distractions of the Roman diaspora. (See Paintner, *Desert Fathers and Mothers: Early Christian Wisdom Sayings*, 2012) See also: David P. Gushee a Sojourners contributing editor. As the Distinguished University Professor of Christian Ethics, Mercer University, Atlanta, he explored the context in which "The Roots of White Supremacist Christianity began in the Empire-building nations of the Colonial Age". His discussion laid out the central purpose of the Doctrine of Discovery: "There was no original innocence. The heresy of racism and its resulting sins were there from the beginning." The analysis of the commitment to perpetual slavery is examined to include the masterminding of the Slave Trade to concentrate on importing African slaves to Europe and the Americas. (See Gushee, "Born in Heresy", Sojourners Magazine, Sept/Oct 2020, Vol. 49 No. 9, sojo.net)

The heresy code enforcement drove many followers of the Jesus lifestyle into exile. Jesus taught his disciples to trust the unconditional love and compassion of God, in whose image we are all created.

The scriptures contained in the Holy Bible introduce us to the Creation of Earth as a continuous event, which will always be the foundation of Earth's lifestyle (see Genesis 1:20-28). In addition, Jesus taught us that God existed in spirit only and surrounds us all in God's outdoor Holy Temple (see the praying of the Lord's Prayer in Chapter 1).

Non-European Christians, such as Coptic Christians in Africa, had separately established their own following of the Risen Christ. The Coptic Orthodox Church split away from the Roman Christian community in 451 A.D. The Coptic Church diverged from other Christians during the 5th century in part due to differing beliefs about the nature of Christ. Coptic Christians believe that Christ had two natures—one human and one divine—"without separation". The Coptic Orthodox Church had brought Christianity to Egypt and founded the Coptic church during the first century. It is in the Middle East and was the first founded in Africa. The mingling, without confusion, and without alteration. Catholics and other Christian denominations believe in the incarnation of Jesus, which similarly holds that Christ was both fully human and fully divine. But at the time of the split, Coptic Christians were accused of believing that Christ had only one, divine nature.

Coptic Christians trace their founding to the Apostle St. Mark. (See: Antonia Blumberg, "Who Are Egypt's Coptic Christians And What do They Believe?", Huffington Post, 4-10-2017)

Emperor Constantine's Roman Church eventually became the Christianity of Europe. At the time, the European lifestyle was based on the forced labor customs of feudalism. In 799 A.D., under Pope Leo III, the Church of Rome became the Holy Roman Empire.

John Wycliffe, a prominent theologian and reformer English leader of the 14th Century, promoted the first English translation of the Bible. Wycliffe was an English theologian, philosopher, church reformer, and promoter of the first complete translation of the Bible into English. (Also spelled Wycliff, Wyclif, Wicliffe, or Wiclif; born c. 1330, England; died December 31, 1384, Lutterworth, Leicestershire.) He was one of the forerunners of the Protestant Reformation. The politico-ecclesiastical theories that he developed required the church to give up its worldly possessions, and in 1378 he began a systematic attack on the beliefs and practices of the church dictated by Roman Catholicism. The Lollards, a "heretical group", propagated his controversial views. (See: Brittanica. com article about John Wycliffe by John Stacey)

The Holy Roman Empire Had a New Challenge

The Holy Roman Empire had inherited the will of Emperor Constantine to render the "things of God" to Caesar. The Emperor wanted to control what his subjects believed. As Emperor and son of his god, he sought to maintain control of the Roman Empire.

However, all of God's created beings are blessed with free will, including the Emperor's subjects. Thus, he had to bully his citizens into obeying the creeds of the Council of Nicaea, without question. This was the direction stated by Pope Nicholas V in 1452, when he led the European invasion of the Americas.

Wycliffe and his followers in England had been exposed to the WORD. They exercised the free will they had inherited, being created in the image of God.

The Reformation movement had begun back in 1378 under the influence of Wycliffe and his followers. However, the Black Death and the War of the Roses against France slowed the next stage of the Wycliffe movement. The Black Death in Europe was the bubonic plague, a pandemic that killed 60% of the European population, from 1347 to 1351. Then in 1455 in the weakened England, Henry V died, leaving the baby Henry VI to the throne. He married an ambitious noble, Margaret of France. Richard of York became a protector of Henry VI. After 30 years of endless skirmishes and the death of Henry VI the throne was secured by Henry VII in 1485.

The King James Bible was published in 1611, during the birth of the modern printing press. It had taken this long for the Wycliffe movement to regain momentum. The printing press was a direct challenge to the European church and the authority of the Holy Roman Empire. It was an opportunity for the churches in England to see, study and discuss the scriptures in their congregations for the first time. This opportunity also fueled a concerted effort to abolish slavery in the colonial empires. England led the growing movement to abolish colonial slavery, as an affront to genuine Christianity as an authentic message from Jesus.

Megan McKenna is an author, storyteller, and theologian, who studied, wrote and learned how to speak the ancient unwritten Aramaic language the way Jesus and his disciples used it in their time. As such, it was spoken and used very much like the prophets of the Old Testament. Richard Rohr borrowed her expertise to convey his deeper meaning of the Sermon on the Mount as it would have been received by his disciples. Richard Rohr considered the Beatitudes in Matthew 5:3-20 as Jesus' appeal to his disciples to support each other, with the spirit of unconditional love and compassion that God showers on us all.

Megan McKenna illustrates that when we read: "Blessed are the peacemakers", it would sound like: "Get up, go ahead, do something, move, you peacemakers, for you shall be called children of God". She continued: "To me this reflects Jesus' words and teachings much more accurately. I can hear him saying: 'Get your hands dirty to build a human society for human beings; otherwise, others will torture and murder the poor, the voiceless, and the powerless.' Christianity is not passive but active, energetic, alive, going beyond despair". From the outdoor perspective, we would pray the Lord's Prayer intentionally, pausing at "thy Kingdom come" to absorb the scene of the Holy Temple in the dome of Heaven depicted in Genesis 1:14-20. As we say "thy will be done" we feel the presence of God surrounding each of us, as God's spirit fills the Temple, and we listen for God's will, to share with each other!

The "American Way" of the USA has made the people of the other Americas foreigners in their own territory. The indigenous people of the Americas were at home in their own God-given territory for tens of thousands of years before the arrival of the Europeans. They lived in cooperative communities, focused on supporting the common good. Their lifestyle was more democratic than anything experienced today in the USA. Moreover, the male-dominant feudal European lifestyle is inherently opposed to universal human dignity and the common good. It eventually gave way to the following colonial attitudes.

As the Inquisitor Francesco Pena reported in 1578, the tyranny of the Inquisition took countless human lives in Europe and around the world. Churchmen also applied religious justification to the widespread practice of slavery. The un-submissive spirit of the Middle Ages only seemed to exacerbate the Church's demand for unquestioning obedience. Their claim was that God had spoken! As the Inquisitor Bernard Gui said, the layman must not argue with the unbeliever, but "thrust his sword into the man's belly as far as it will go." In that time new ideas about spirituality were emerging in England and elsewhere. Pope Innocent III declared "that anyone who attempted to construe a personal view of God which conflicted with Church dogma must be burned without pity." (See also: Irenaeus, of Lyons (author), "Saint Irenaeus: Against Heresies Paperback," Editors: Alexander Robert, James Donaldson, A. Cleveland, Ex Fontibus Company, March 28, 2012; Slick, Matt, "Heresy", the Christian Apologetics and Research Ministry, Counterblast, 2006-8; Ellerbe, Helen, "The Dark Side of Christian History: The Inquisition and Slavery", Morningstar and Lark, 1995)

The Doctrine of Discovery was created to emphasize the European Christian belief that they were direct descendants of the people of the Old Testament, who they believed to be European. This boosted their sense of religious entitlement to manage the perpetual slavery of non-Europeans in the colonies. This concept of European supremacy has continued to drive a painful heresy. The journey from Jesus to the popular Christ of today is explained in the Public Broadcasting Service (PBS) Frontline documentary "From Jesus to Christ". (April 1998. Frontline ©1995- 2014, WGBH Educational Foundation)

This history of early Christianity covers the period from the life of Jesus to the First Council of Nicaea in 325. The range and variety of people and groups, who sought to follow the commission of Jesus baffled Irenaeus and his followers for decades. The complexity of the belief systems of the diverse groups in the Jesus movement could not be enforced. This dilemma is well presented in the above mentioned documentary, "From Jesus to Christ".

Jesus Introduced His Disciples to God's Outdoor Holy Temple

Both the Nicene Creed and the Apostles Creed taught the followers of the Church of Rome that Jesus is seated at the right hand of the Father. That frames a European indoor Christianity, with God depicted as "the man upstairs".

According to Jesus, the Father is spirit. In God's Holy Temple the spirit of God fills the entire cosmos. Thus, there cannot be a right hand of the Spirit in God's Holy Temple. Furthermore, Genesis 1:14-20 introduces us to the dome of the sky, which is the heaven that surrounds everyone. In other words, no one can escape the presence of God!

The churches that champion exclusive male dominant leadership do not honor the fact that God is equally male and female (Genesis 1:27). Often, the women are the ones in such congregations most likely to share with Jesus the carrying of his yoke (Matthew 11:28-30).

In addition, the liturgical and eucharistic accounts of Good Friday and the Easter Resurrection in today's churches seldom portray the unique role of the female disciples of Jesus, who remained with Jesus throughout the most devastating part of his ordeal. They were the best source of details of his torture and abuse during the trial and his most humiliating brutality — carrying the cross. Thus, *they* provided the covenant version of the Good Friday passion and the Resurrection.

The outdoor perspective of a dark night, away from the light pollution of most modern cities is particularly dramatic. One can see deep into the heavens at night. Stars are thousands of light-years away. A light year is 9,460,000,000,000,000 km! Our sun is 150,000,000 km away. A light year is 50,000,000 times the distance to the sun.

God in spirit is everywhere at once. Furthermore, God's creation is continuous. Psalm 104 celebrates the splendor of God in ways that make it natural to worship God outdoors, in God's Holy Temple.

The Colonial Era, in addition, celebrates a derogatory relationship to the land. The "rulers of creation" felt entitled to their role as slave masters. Thus, they related to the land as if it were "God's footstool".

There were slaves who valued the land as if it offered them kinship. This was shown in the Carter Museum in Atlanta, Georgia. The museum did not glorify slavery. However, it demonstrated how a slave sometimes created his (or her) sense of stewardship. Most of his time was devoted to working on the master's plantation. In addition, a slave garden was sometimes cultivated on a small plot next to a slave's hut (about 200 square feet) which he carefully tended when he had time.

Christ-Like vs. Christian

In the effort to support the natural indigenous matriarchal customs in Alaska, Eastern orthodox missionaries called their mission "Christ-like". In that spirit, they sought to clearly reflect the authentic teachings and life of Jesus. For instance, they recruited mothers as their primary native leaders because in that culture their communal care for their village children made them naturally Christ-like. In such villages, many fathers joined in to care for both mothers and children.

Jesus said on many occasions that one needs to come as a child in order to enter the kingdom of heaven. When I garden with my Mayan forest farmer friend in Belize, I am struck by the way he becomes like a little child as he relates to his garden. He also shifts into that childlike consciousness when he comes to help me in my garden.

In such stewardship, he listens as a child to the voice of God coming from Earth. This attribute is common among most indigenous cultures in the Americas and globally. As in the time of Jesus, people patiently interacted with each other. The entire village adapted to the pace of life of the congregation of mothers accommodating the immediate needs of the village's children.

When Emperor Constantine Rendered Unto Caesar What is God's He Still Could Not Control It

The Church of Rome under Pope Leo III named the Empire "The Holy Roman Empire" in 799. A succession of popes ruled the Holy Roman Empire, as Rome gained control over Europe. In 1452 Pope Nicholas V initiated control over the Americas, when he issued the Doctrine of Discovery.

In 1789 the United States of America gained independence from Britain. Soon the United States became known to the other European states as "America". In the spirit of its society the other countries of the Americas were regarded as foreigners in their own land, especially after the Spanish American War of 1898.

By this time European supremacy had become firmly established throughout the Americas. The indigenous populations had been displaced. In most cases, the indigenous settlers had been made landless foreigners in the lands that their ancestors had occupied for tens of thousands of years before the arrival of the first Europeans.

Between 2017 and 2021 the USA had been led by President Trump, whose most persistent system of government had been geared to persecute non-Europeans. Many Christian leaders spoke out against the Trump administration. Jim Wallis, publisher of Sojourner Magazine compared it to Hitler's Germany. In his study of Dietrich Bonhoeffer, a young pastor and theologian in Germany during the rise of Adolf Hitler, he suggested that the key questions of that study were as relevant to President Trump in 2020 as they were to Hitler in 1930.

Bonhoeffer had founded an underground seminary, where he helped to lead what became known as the Confessing Church. His fundamental question was always, "Who is Jesus Christ for us today?" First, Truth is a central Christian concern. Many presidents have lied when it served their political interests. In the Trump administration, lying has become persistent and pathological, occurring almost every day from the White House and the daily press briefing. No administration is ever happy with its press coverage, but the Trump administration regularly presents the honest media coverage as "fake news". This is a dangerous assault on freedom of the press and the First Amendment.

Second, the President readily celebrates racial bigotry, another central Christian concern. From Trump's "birtherism" that questioned the identity of the first black president to his attacks on Mexican immigrants, from his Muslim bans to his appeals to white nationalism, Trump has used racial fear and hate to his political advantage. Thus, he has supported the racial divide in the church. We in the Jesus discipleship are suffering while parts of the body of Christ feel the pain of his non-European victims, including the strangers, immigrants and refugees among us.

Third, Trump's strongman style of leadership is a direct contradiction of the Christian ethic of servant leadership, and the civic ethic of public service, and points to the critical need for equal human constitutional leadership promised by our political leaders.

Fourth, "America First" is a theological heresy. The body of Christ is the most racially and culturally diverse community on Earth – our connection to brothers and sisters all over the world makes our political convictions global, and not just national. And stewardship of the Earth, its resources and its people, is a priority for people of faith over an administration that shows no concern for God's creation.

The Trump Administration disregarded the fact that the population of US citizens makes it probably the most cosmopolitan country on Earth. His focus was on segregating and persecuting all non-Europeans, who are now about 40% of the US population and over 70% of the population of the Americas.

Young citizens seeking a more responsible administration for their own future voted for Joe Biden to replace President Trump. Many also sought to heal the effects of the climate crisis and to gain control of the rapidly increasing coronavirus death spiral in the USA. By October 2021 these deaths had surpassed 700,000.

In this context, consider the personal voice of a voting young person:

> I'm Thuy, a female, Asian-American college student at Tulane University. My parents are Vietnamese immigrants who never attended college and always worked in the labor market. They've always stressed to me, "Work hard to get a degree, don't get distracted, focus, and study hard."
>
> Growing up, I lived as an American teenager by day and a Vietnamese daughter by night. That cultural tension left me struggling to understand my own personal ideals and values. As I got older, I wanted to explore my romantic life, just like anyone else. I worried though that (I would be met with judgement) it might be a distraction from my studies. How could I possibly date knowing that my parents' worst nightmare was

having my education jeopardized in any way? Coming from a low-income family, my parents hoped that one of their children might land a lucrative career as a doctor, lawyer, or engineer. Where did my love life fit into that dream?

Two years ago, I decided to explore my birth control options so that I could be protected from pregnancy while dating and continuing my education. I arrived at Planned Parenthood fresh out of high school with a 4.0 GPA, my Medicaid insurance card, and my future in my back pocket. As a patient, I was thoroughly educated on my options with care and privacy. I learned that I have control over my own body and can make the best decisions for myself — just between me and my doctor.

I was able to access care thanks to Medicaid, a program that receives funding based on census information. That's why it is so important to fill out the 2020 Census. Census numbers help to dictate funding for other programs like Medicaid, upon which me and many of my peers rely. It is also imperative that we have our voices heard at the ballot box. Voting ensures my voice is being represented by members of Congress.

I'm so proud to stand with Planned Parenthood, which not only provides health care but works to make sure people like me and my family are filling out the census and getting registered to vote.

Civic engagement is important to my community. Certain populations, like families with young children, families with low incomes, immigrants, and Indigenous populations, have historically been underrepresented in census data.

Let Us Reflect on the Easter Celebration by the Risen Christ

The Jesus lifestyle and his desire for the well-being of his disciples had a distinctly different emphasis from the European Christianity we have inherited. Following his resurrection Jesus was emphatic. Jesus sent us out to live into the ultimate promise of Easter.

In his last words the Resurrected Christ said:

- "Greetings! It is great to see you! Welcome!"

- "Fear not! You have nothing to fear!"

- "Peace be onto you! My peace I give you to share with all you meet!"

- "Receive the Holy Spirit! It will always be your comforter!"

- "Believe in me and trust that I am with you always!"

- "As I have forgiven, you are to forgive others. Heal the sick, be present in their grief and sorrow. Heal the broken-hearted."

- "Take up your cross and follow me!"

- "Feed my people and Love everyone, as I have loved you!"

- "As I return to the Father, Go in peace to love and serve the Lord!"

- "I leave you with my blessings and I will be with you always!"

Rev. Richard Singleton presents a compelling account of the last words of the Risen Christ, as he gave his disciples their final instructions to take the show on the road. (See: Richard O. Singleton, *The Last Words of the Resurrected Christ*, 1997)

Most of all, we must remember that Jesus said each of us needs to become like a little child to enter the Kingdom of Heaven. Why? Because little children are always asking questions. They naturally pursue the spirit of lifelong learning. In God's Holy Temple, knowledge is infinite. There is always something more to learn. God is speaking to each of us continually. The male-dominant Caesar sits atop his pyramid, monarch of all he can survey, waiting for his slaves beneath to carry his pyramid. They cannot!

Chapter 7
A Lasting View of the Jesus Lifestyle

"Your sins are forgiven! Come, follow me!"

The Jesus lifestyle is committed to cooperative living. He taught his disciples to pray The Lord's Prayer: "Our Father!" Jesus was devoted to his disciples. Thus, he shared himself freely with them, so that they would seek to live like him. The yoke he gave them all to carry called them to share their life with each other in the spirit of God's unconditional love and compassion. This most fundamental truth is the central foundation of his discipleship. To appreciate such a lifestyle, we need to share our personal lives with each other the way Jesus shared himself with his disciples outdoors in God's Holy Temple.

In the spirit of the child, we would be obsessed with exploring the new experience of living outside the womb. The European lifestyle has enforced an artificial indoor civilization, which it calls Christianity. This enforcement demands that its subjects live exclusively within this religious lifestyle.

However, Jesus calls his disciples to thirst for lifelong learning as we explore God's Holy Temple. The infinity of the spirit that is the WORD gives way to a mantra of perpetual exploration of the Spirit of God in God's Holy Temple.

The Doctrine of Discovery promoted the religion which Emperor Constantine promoted in the pagan ritual of the Roman Empire. This religion has promoted almost 600 years of colonial abuse in a slave-centered civilization. It is also a religion of rapid activity without thinking of the continuous unconditional love of God that requires us all to live at the slow and deliberate "godspeed" that Moses demonstrated in his capacity to notice that the burning bush was not being consumed. We simply need to slow down to "godspeed".

God made us human beings in the image of God. We have become "human doings" in our current lifestyle. Furthermore, at our customary pace of life, we are no longer in tune with much of what we do in such haste. In effect, we live in a subconscious mind and seldom in our hearts, where genuine love presides.

The Discomfort of Such a Frantic Lifestyle in a World Divorced from the Common Good

Today we are witnessing the greatest proportion of refugees in our world population. An alarming aspect of this misdirection has been outlined in the findings of Doctors Without Borders, published in its Fall 2017 *Alert*, vol. 18 no. 3. This report presents their global assessment of a rapidly expanding refugee crisis.

Their MSF Report of outpatient treatment activities (Medecins Sans Frontierres) is globally recognized. It highlights the urgently global threat to women fleeing from sexual rape and related abuse. Most of these refugees have been subjected to gang rape episodes, in which women are crowded into an area at gunpoint and forced to watch while many of them are being gang-raped. As disciples of Jesus, we all need to slow down to "godspeed" and give ourselves the time necessary to digest what is happening here. This is a yoke which Jesus wants to share with anyone, who cares to follow him!

Jesus calls us to live from the heart, sharing the unconditional love and compassion of God. The scale of the MSF report challenges the disciples of Jesus to share the related pain and suffering hereby portrayed. The report needs to be digested in the spirit of God's love and compassion.

Over 500,000 are fleeing their homes in Central America. More than 422,000 Rohingya refugees crossed into Bangladesh from Myanmar. In Nigeria, the conflict between Boko Haram and regional armed attack created 2.5 million refugees, who are subjected to a wide range of abuses, led by sexual assaults. One million fled into Uganda from the South

Sudan conflict. They were placed in four refugee camps. In the Democratic Republic, Congo 270,000 outpatients visited one site. Others were treated on the run. In the outskirts of Syria 372,700 outpatients were treated amid escalated violence. The clinic concentrates on treating the children among the fleeing families. In the war-torn region of Afghanistan, they served 328,100 outpatients.

Consider the plight of women subjected to rape and torture. In many instances, mothers and daughters are together, sisters, cousins, classmates, neighbors. They flee at the earliest opportunity. MSF activities have taken refugees to Europe where the MSF serve refugee camps.

In the USA, as in most parts of the world women do not report these abuses, since they tend to be considered the criminals to be "stoned to death"! The MSF staff are well trained to be appropriately compassionate. (See: The Doctors Without Borders MSF Report, (Medecins Sans Frontierres), Fall 2017 *Alert*, vol 18, no. 3)

The Time Has Come for a New Christianity of The Jesus Lifestyle

Jesus taught his disciples to help him in carrying his yoke. In ***praying*** the Lord's Prayer they learned to love and worship the God of unconditional love and compassion. In this spirit, we are called to serve the common good in response to the Doctors Without Borders appeal. We see evidence of their findings in large urban settlements globally. ***This appeal can no longer be ignored!***

We should pray together with other disciples as often as possible. We must together listen to God in the spirit of the covenant that Abraham established with God. The agreement was that each successive descendant of Abraham would share the collective messages we receive from God.

Because his disciples prayed together, it became natural for some of them to share a collective caring for their neighbor. In so doing, Jesus gave us two specific commandments: You shall love the Lord, your God with all your heart and with all your soul and with all your mind. This is the greatest and first commandment. And the second is like it: you should love your neighbor as yourself. On these commandments hang all the law and the prophets (Matthew 22:37-40). As such, Jesus called them to share the unconditional love and compassion that comes from God.

Praying to the God we worship is personal and intimate. It is also relation-building, between each of us and God and with each other in the presence of God. The nature of such prayer is communal. It invites us continually into the spirit of Abraham's covenant with the Father (see Chapter 3).

Advent is the Beginning of the European Church Year

In Advent, the baby Jesus invites us all to become like a child. The Hebrew tradition begins with the call: "Oh! come, Oh! Come Emanuel, and ransom captive Israel!" The Advent season calls the church community to prepare for a sacred Christmas season. These prophets were crying out to God to send healing to the lost community of Israel. Advent is God's response to their desperate call for healing. Advent prepares us to receive Jesus out of a deep longing, (listen to the song of Mary, mother of Jesus in Luke 1:46-56).

Beginning on December 25 we are supposed to celebrate the 12 days of the Christmas season (from 25 December to 5 January). On 6 January, the Epiphany celebrates what the coming of Jesus means to the life of all created in the image of God, as we pray the Lord's Prayer together.

Jesus Calls Us to an Advent Entirely Different from the Colonial Advent We Inherited

The prophets of the Old Testament called Israel to lament and sing: "Oh Come Emanuel and ransom captive Israel!"

In the spirit of Abraham's covenant with God, we need to slow down to allow for the space and time necessary to contemplate our joint effort to receive Jesus, as a group praying the Lord's Prayer together. In this way, today's disciples of Jesus would contemplate Advent as a period of appropriate preparation. We cannot adapt the Christianity we have inherited to such a task. We sincerely need to build a new community, based on the Jesus lifestyle (see Chapter 3).

In that respect, we should become like the honest child within each of us. In that spirit, we welcome Jesus, the child, at Christmas. As we pray: "thy Kingdom come!", in the Lord's Prayer, we worship the God, who is inviting us into the continuing creation, in the spirit of the covenant. We are in no hurry!

Such a spirit can lead us to combine the Buddhist Economics concept of shared community building with the reconciliation spirit of Ubuntu theology promoted by Archbishop Tutu. He shared this spirit of deep love during his special celebration of global love with The Dalai Lama.

His Holiness the Dalai Lama and Archbishop Desmond Tutu, in collaboration with Douglas Abrams discussed the concept of caring for each other in community. Based on the spirit of contagious kindness, they practice generous forgiveness to enhance one's spontaneous feeling of compassion for others. (See: Douglas Abrams, The Dalai Lama and Archbishop Desmond Tutu, *The Book of Joy: Lasting Happiness in a*

Changing World, 2016. Also: Pema Chodron, *When Things Fall Apart: Heart Advice for Difficult Times*, 1997)

Worshiping God in God's Holy Temple

When we seek to worship God in God's Holy Temple, we see the splendor of God (Psalm 104) in ever growing magnitude. Dori Grinenko Baker, in her book *Greenhouses of Hope*, encouraged the young people with whom she interacted to pray together with and for each other as discussed in Chapter 5.

Consider the Spiritual Impact of European Christianity on a Multitude of Colonial Subjects

The colonial legacy cannot be ignored. The European Christian movement was powerful in teaching such a compromising false image of God for almost 1800 years.

The account of a young woman, who lived through the genocide that killed most of her immediate family, many of her neighbors, her village and most of the people in her life offers a unique feeling of empathy that grows out of gratitude for the God who strengthened them through such an ordeal. In 1994, Immaculee Ilibagiza escaped to the house of a neighbor and close friend of the family. At great risk to himself and his family, this priest, a member of the other Rwanda group committing the genocide hid her and seven other women in a small inner bathroom toilet stall for three months.

Immaculee survived the entire experience in prayer. It was such a painful experience that it took her over ten years to write her book. She collected and compiled a vivid account of her ordeal, which is summarized in her book from extensive volumes of notes, which details what she prayed. She managed to hold onto the red and white rosary which was the last thing her father gave her as he sent her off to his trusted friend to be protected. Her prayers guided her to make strategic decisions that saved her life on many occasions. These prayers taught her to forgive. In the end, she told someone, who was encouraging her to punish former genocide perpetrators: "Forgiveness is all I have to offer!" (See: Immaculee Ilibagiza, *Left to Tell: Discovering God Amidst the Rwandan Holocaust*, 2006)

It would be easy to bask in the happy ending of Immaculee's story, but that would defeat the more critical purpose of her journey. Here is one of many examples of the colonial abuse of European Christianity on innocent children of God in their native land, which God had given them.

The Belgian colonists had cultivated brutal prejudice in Rwanda. They generalized the facial features of the Hutus as having broad flat noses and the Tutsis having high nose bridges. They proceeded to periodically instigate major conflict between the two groups.

Following the conflict in 1959, the larger community resumed their normal non-colonial lifestyle. Many old acquaintances had reconnected and inter-married. Thus, generalized features became blurred. During the 1980s, the Hutus were being given free license to exterminate the Tutsis.

In the 1990s I had a spiritual director who knew Immaculee personally and loaned me a copy of her book. I purchased my own copy and came to appreciate more deeply how much of her faith had grown through her willingness to trust in the sufficiency of the love of God for her life. She truly believed that God was saving her to tell her story!

She talks about being outdoors in the first weeks of her eventual rescue, when she gathered with a small group of missing friends, with whom she could share her ordeal. She appreciated the feeling of worshiping God in God's Holy Temple and being lifted from the trauma in her first helicopter ride.

The USA Continues to Abuse the Americas

The recent attempted coup by President Trump may have distracted from a deeper evil that few seem to appreciate in the USA. In continuing to refer to themselves as "Americans", the

USA systematically denies the rightful identity of hundreds of millions of other Americans in the Americas.

The True Americans

The geography of the Americas ratifies the continent of North and South America as the Americas. The area we call Central America is the southern part of North America. It is true that the Panama Canal was built to shorten the trip from the East coast of the USA to the West coast. It is also true that North and South America are geographically connected. The Panama Canal would naturally close itself if routine maintenance were not continued to keep it open. Such is the nature of Earth's lifestyle.

The Cost of Violating the Global Truth of Earth's Lifestyle

Large countries, such as China, India, Russia, Australia and Brazil make decisions that have global impacts. They have similarly violated natural truth. The coronavirus pandemic seems to be a product of decisions made by these large countries.

The European Christian phenomenon often works in subtle, familiar settings: (see below, reference to Pat Marrin's article on "Women Disciples"). In his article, he demonstrates that "a different Gospel lies almost hidden in the midst of the one we have".

What survives from Luke's simple account is a description of the band of disciples accompanying Jesus as both men and women traveling together. Even taking into account cultural and historical differences, this display of humanity supports the idea that Jesus wanted his movement to show how God's grace made real community possible, excluding no one. The idea of male-only church leadership was not a part of the Jesus lifestyle. The women played a key role, remaining faithful to Jesus to the end and serving as the first witnesses to his resurrection. (See: "Women disciples", Pencil Preaching for Friday, September 20, 2019, National Catholic Reporter, Sep 19, 2019, by Pat Marrin)

"Accompanying Jesus were the Twelve and some women who had been cured of evil spirits and infirmities" (Luke 8:2).

The Young Voices in Our Community

The way Greta Thunberg has brought us to care for future generations encourages my village to raise our children in the spirit of the Advent story of the arrival of God, the child. We need to call each other to Greta's movement to help map out the best ways forward in harmony with Earth's lifestyle.

Secretary-General António Guterres still urges countries to keep sight of the global warming challenge, as we confront the coronavirus pandemic. The Secretary General made it clear that all UN resources for now would be directed toward tackling the coronavirus pandemic crisis. "The control of the coronavirus pandemic is now the world's top priority. The climate crisis will have to be put on the back burner, for now". He urged countries to not lose sight of the global warming challenge and the Paris climate accord (Reported by Nathanial Gronewold, E&E News on March 23, 2020).

The Larger Message of the Late Bill Withers – "Lean On Me"

In the wake of the coronavirus pandemic the death of Bill Withers in early April prompted this song to be played in his memory. The song was a comfort for many.

Here is the beginning of the song by Bill Withers, "Lean On Me":

> *Sometimes in our lives we all have pain*
> *We all have sorrow*
> *But if we are wise*
> *We know that there's always tomorrow*

Lean on me, when you're not strong
And I'll be your friend
I'll help you carry on
For it won't be long
'Til I'm gonna need
Somebody to lean on

[The rest of the lyrics can be found on the internet]

The song contains the message that Jesus gives his disciples when he calls on them to take his heavy yoke and make it light by carrying it together (Matthew 11: 28-30).

God speaks to each of us in different ways. During the early months of the coronavirus pandemic, the Bill Withers lyrics supported our collective need to care for each other through the pandemic.

Chapter 8
It Takes a Village to Raise a Child

Most indigenous people live in villages all over this Earth. They live the "village" lifestyle, which is cooperative. Such is their reality. Their villages were generally led by the mothers raising the children together. They raised the male and female children together with a demonstrated equality that encouraged the older children to care for the younger ones.

The scriptures honored such cooperative communities throughout, beginning with Genesis 1:14-20. God's Holy Temple is outdoors. Heaven is the dome of the sky, which **surrounds us all**.

Jesus impressed his disciples with his lifestyle. As a trusted rabbi, they were so impressed that they asked him to teach them to pray (Luke 11:1-13). As most people at this time did not have access to the written word, their prayer together relied on the eye-to-eye, heart-to-heart intimacy inherent to the Old Testament. Accordingly, the Old Testament narrative included extensive repetition.

In Genesis 1:14-20 we see something unique about the heavens. The days have greater light, while the nights give us lesser light. By night light, we can see, at greater depth, the stars that are light-years from the Earth. A light-year is over a million times the distance from Earth to the sun. One needs to take this time to worship this image of God as spirit. The spirit of God fills the entire cosmos. As such, wherever I am, I am surrounded by God. The European concept of God as "the man upstairs" lacks such imagery. Praying the Lord's Prayer together draws us into the communal spirit of the covenant God made with Abraham (see Chapter 3). Jesus was teaching that covenant to his lost Jewish community throughout his presence on Earth. In effect, the covenant that God had made with Abraham explained that each successive descendant of Abraham would develop a slightly different relationship with God, which was to be incorporated into the covenant.

The Sermon on the Mount provides an example of his appeal to his disciples to look after each other (see Chapter 3). It was his outline of the Beatitudes. He describes the weaknesses of his disciples and shows how these become blessings, when they serve each other. Thus, Jesus invites his disciples to help him carry his yoke (Matthew 11:25-30). Jesus shares with them his concept of "being gentle and humble in heart". Such sharing brings "rest to your soul" (v. 29). Thus, whatever we ask "in his name" will be granted.

Furthermore, Jesus calls his disciples to enter the Kingdom of Heaven as a little child. As such, it takes a village to raise a child. It was such a community of mothers who brought the children to Jesus to be blessed (see Matthew 18:1-5) The collective of mothers leading the village enable it to become worthy of the child!

The cooperative lifestyle of the village echoes the golden rule: "love your neighbor as yourself". One wishes for his/her neighbor what one would like for self. In other words, the love of self is essential in cooperative living. Self-sacrifice is not regarded as a goal of such cooperative living. In this respect, learning to love self becomes a lifelong learning task. The co-operative lifestyle facilitates such learning.

The Gospel of John takes us directly to the relationship between Jesus and God, the Father. "In the beginning was the Word. The Word was with God and the Word was God!" (John 1:1-2). The introduction continues to explain John the Baptist and his role in paving the way for Jesus to begin his ministry to the children of Abraham (John 1:1-18).

Jesus emphasizes the village raising the child when he meets the woman at the well (John 4:24), when he tells her: "God is spirit and those, who worship him must worship in spirit and truth". So critical is the nature and context of that worship that

Jesus takes his disciples to spend two days with the woman and her community teaching them to live in community and be the village equipped to raise their children (see John 4:7-42).

European Christianity is Built on Heresy

European colonial Christianity has been built on the heresy that Europeans are direct descendants of Jesus, who they claim to have been European. The truth is that Jesus is a Jew, a descendant of Abraham, born into the household of Joseph, a descendant of Abraham. There were no cameras in those days. Europe was an isolated settlement, in which few had seen people who did not look like them. Accordingly, when they sought to illustrate the story of Christianity, the people in their story were painted as Europeans.

At the Council of Nicaea in 352 AD Emperor Constantine made the Church of Rome a department of the Roman Empire. Pope Leo III made the Church the Holy Roman Empire in 799 AD (see Introduction). When Pope Nicholas V announced the expansion of European Christianity into the Americas, he introduced the slavery of all non-Europeans as a religious rite of European Christianity.

This was a second heresy. In the Beatitudes of Matthew 5:3-20, Jesus described to his disciples how their weaknesses were actually blessings to each other, as they provided tangible reasons why they served each other, as he required of them.

As Rabbi Jesus, he was continually teaching them parables to illustrate to them how to be continual blessings to each other. In fact, he impressed on them that he called them to help him carry his yoke, Matthew 11: 25-30, to make it lighter. The parable of the prodigal son was one such lesson. The young son had taken his share of his father's fortune and lost it all. But he did not cease to be his father's son and had been forgiven. The older son had remained faithful and all that he had built with his father was his. Thus, he invited the faithful son to welcome his brother back into the household, which was also his.

In another instant, Jesus reminded Martha that she and Mary had chosen two different ways to welcome him. When we serve God, we do not try to weigh the value of the service. God shows us unconditional love with compassion to share with everyone.

In the parable of the Good Samaritan, Jesus reminds his disciples that sometimes the one you least expect will turn up to rescue you from disaster. That is another reason why you love your neighbor as yourself. Furthermore, it is the bigger reason why one needs to learn to love self as much as God loves you, who are created in the image of God!

With the incident of the woman caught in adultery, Jesus ridicules the popular habit of male dominance. He also reminds us that the image of God is both female and male. The deeper calling is to be honest about God's genuine love for each of us.

Which man was not born of a woman, who usually nurtured him to the point of basic maturity? When one genuinely **prays** the Lord's Prayer, it should be an act of worship to the God, who loves us all unconditionally, with endless compassion.

Listening to God

The Christians, whose custom is to recite prescribed prayers, in the spirit of colonial Christianity tend to relate to God as the object of their entitlement. Howard Thurman encouraged his listeners to speak directly to God as the specific focus of their engagement. He explains that Jesus had resented deeply the loss of Jewish independence and the aggression of Rome. The balm of that burning humiliation was humility.... Thus, Jesus asked his people to learn from him, "For I am meek and lowly in heart; and ye shall find rest upon your souls. For my yoke is easy and my burden is light". See Matthew 11:29-30. (See: Howard Thurman, *Jesus and the Disinherited*, 1976)

Against this backdrop, it is critical that we keep our focus on the authentic Jesus lifestyle. The global refugee crisis reported by The Doctors Without Borders MSF Report, in the previous chapter, must motivate us all to appropriate action in the name of Jesus. Howard Thurman, in his discussion with victims of European Christianity, helps many to see and feel the more inclusive power of Abraham's covenant with God.

Grace Before Meals

It is generally a passive prayer we were taught to say. However, when I know who grew the food I am eating and how it was grown, my grace seldom acknowledges the persons who prepared my meal. The food from the supermarket would have involved hundreds to thousands of workers, most of whom are generally under-paid and overworked. Jesus calls me, as his disciples, to acknowledge all my neighbors who serve me.

In our economy the urban poor are forced into a money economy at an overwhelming disadvantage. Their minimum wages are often less than half the value of a living wage. We need to take the time to know their pain and suffering and share such awareness with Jesus in prayer!

Jim Wallis, in his book, *America's Original Sin*, hints at such sharing. He invited Bryan Stevenson to write a foreword to his work. In this foreword, Stevenson, the author of *Just Mercy*, describes two separate incidents in which he was attacked and almost killed, merely because he is African American. His closing remark underlines the role we need to play to bring Abraham's covenant into focus, as we seek to be disciples of Jesus. Stevenson writes: "No historic presidential election, no athlete or entertainer's success, no silent tolerance of one another is enough to create the truth and reconciliation needed to eliminate racial inequality or the presumption of guilt. We're going to have to collectively acknowledge our failures at dealing with racial bias. People of faith are going to have to raise their voices and take action." (See foreword: Jim Wallis, *America's Original Sin: Racism, White Privilege and the Bridge to a New America*, 2016)

Jim Wallis was writing this book in the wake of the 17 June 2015 shooting of participants at the sanctuary of historic Emanuel African Methodist Episcopal (AME) Church in Charleston, South Carolina. The spirit of the Americanism of the USA is persistent in its fundamental pursuit of our racism pandemic.

In his concept of "Dying to Whiteness" Jim Wallis echoes much of the thesis of Howard Thurman. It underlines the desperate need of each US Christian to be transformed into a new person to follow Jesus as his disciple. The Jesus lifestyle is one of listening directly to God and following what one hears. His invitation to help carry his yoke indicates that we belong to each other. We are all created in the image of God. As such, the pandemic of forced racism is a violation of the covenant and God's purpose.

Joan Chittister's book, *The Time is Now: A Call to Uncommon Courage*, outlines the role taken on by the prophets of the Old Testament. She stresses the urgency of the Church of God's followers to be transformed into disciples of the Jesus lifestyle. In her Chapter 5, she outlines the audacity it takes to break with the dogma of the established religion and seek to follow the authentic leadership of Jesus. Throughout the next 13 chapters she builds the case for systematically preparing oneself to become a prophet in our own time, as true disciples of Jesus. The combination of elements that evolve from a community committed to serving the needs of its members enables one to get to know the intimate needs of one's neighbors. Such love and caring are contagious. It becomes the soul of the community. People give without thinking of possible rewards. I do not need to anticipate my own needs, because someone else is caring for me. It all makes the yoke feel light. (See: Joan Chittister, *The Time is Now: A Call to Uncommon Courage*, 2019)

Jim Wallis has been the editor of the monthly magazine, "Sojourners", for decades. It has been a continuing source of inspiration in my discipleship. The Sept-Oct 2014 edition features soldiers returning from the wars in Iraq and Afghanistan "in unprecedented numbers with post-traumatic stress". The cover story portrays Vonita Murray on her farm near Sacramento, California, not far from my own home in Richmond,

California. She and several other veterans describe the deep healing they experience in the process of engaging family and friends in planting and growing food to feed their poor and hungry neighbors.

As in the healing lifestyle described by Joan Chittister above, the veterans were finding that farming took their post-traumatic stress from the past pain of war into the future promise of feeding their community. That was their intimate healing therapy, healing both them and their neighbors!

J. Philip Newell, in his book *Christ of the Celts*, describes a deeper sense of distraction in the teachings of Jesus, which he calls: "the healing of creation". Celtic Christianity follows the Abraham covenant, indulging in the unconditional love and compassion of the WORD. It is like the post-traumatic stress of the soldiers described above. It also is personal to me, since I am currently studying the works of Pierre Teilhard de Chardin and St. Ignatius of Loyola.

In this chapter he is describing the findings of Pierre Teilhard de Chardin, who was assigned to China by his superiors, hoping to discourage his paleontology. It was at the time archaeologists had discovered the human origins of "Peking Man", which was 500,000 years old. A strong Celtic belief is that God speaks to us through the Creation. Pierre saw the oneness of God and the Creation as parts of a whole unbroken reality into which Jesus invited us to participate. Eastern mysticism helps us indulge in this relationship with God and the continuous Creation. Jesus tells us, as his disciples: "Your sins are forgiven. Come, follow me and share my yoke. Love one another as I have loved you. Do this in remembrance of me and there would be very little room left for sin"!

The Pain and Suffering of Children in Today's Urban Societies Often Needs Special Attention

In the USA, especially in low-income communities, children count on school meals for their only predictable daily food intake. Navy veteran, Kelly Carlisle is an African American from East Oakland. She got a group of neighborhood children to play together and learn the skills they would need to be hired into youth jobs that hire young people after-school during the school year. She found out at the end of her training that no one would hire them, because "people say the whole area is 'unhireable'!" Given such fundamental bigotry in many established USA communities, the New Church will need to portray the Jesus lifestyle at new levels of yoke-sharing.

Good Teachers Often Learn a Great Deal from Their Students

The late Dr. Clarence Jackson, Director of the State Department of Education, California shared with me the sense that good teachers are instinctively better learners. He was my best mentor. As such, he impressed on me the will to seek to learn from my students. Teaching at the community college level offered me a stream of such opportunities:

- A retired airline pilot explained the complex flow patterns of the Jet Stream in the upper atmosphere that enabled pilots to use or avoid to their benefit.

- Another student took me to meet his father, who had managed to escape a massacre in his village in El Salvador with the few of his family survivors. (See: Julio Leiva, *El Terco Deseo de Crear: Un Mejor Mañana*, 2005)

- Another student, an electrician, explained the accidents he survived and the precautions he learned while installing solar panels on his roof.

- Still another student was upset by his term project,

which revealed to him the floating plastic materials in the oceans twice the size of Texas. Thus, he got the class to join him in recycling plastic bags to reduce our collective impact in contributing plastic material to the oceans.

Sharing the yoke with Jesus as his disciple inevitably brings each of us to a lifestyle that recognizes the pain and suffering of our neighbor. I was born and grew up in Trinidad and Tobago, which was a colony of Britain during my elementary school years. The country gained independence while I was in secondary school. As such, I was quite ignorant of the terrorism of African Americans growing up in the USA. Receiving the Equal Justice Initiative 2021 calendar in July 2021 was a rude personal awakening. It slowly took me months of meditation in the spirit of God's unconditional love and compassion to appreciate the yoke Jesus is suffering with millions of African Americans, who are also carrying the yoke with Jesus.

It has taken me many months of meditation, actively listening to children, including preschool children, to feel the pain and suffering that colonialism has loaded on non-Europeans living in the colonies. Colonized parents were also listening to their children. When I meditate on the fact that God and Jesus are also listening it has strengthened the scope of my growing discipleship. I continue to expand my commitment to the covenant that God made with Abraham. (See: *Equal Justice Initiative: A History of Racial Injustice*, 2021 Calendar, Stop Police Killings, 2020, Montgomery, Alabama, eji.org)

Jesus invited his disciples to treat every living soul on God's Earth as their neighbor. These include the plants and animals around us, who are all created in the image of God, the Spirit. The USA, who advertises its nation as a Christian democracy, has violated the image of God and inflicted on the other Americas a range of genocidal evils too painful to ignore.

Rigoberta Menchu, 1992 Nobel Prize Laureate wrote the Foreword to Endangered Peoples. The document illustrates the ongoing process that continues the genocidal termination of Indigenous peoples throughout the world by large countries seeking to intimidate smaller communities within their respective countries. The USA is actively displacing the Indigenous Peoples of the Americas. The Sierra Club Books of San Francisco has published a large picture book called *Endangered Peoples*. (*Endangered Peoples*. Text copyright by Art Davidson, 1993, and photograph copyright by Art Wolfe and John Isaac, 1993)

During the winter of 2021 a group of Indigenous victims gave voice to their struggles. They are: Indigenous Women of the Americas, Defenders of Mother Earth Treaty Compact 2015. They celebrated their continuous compact with their land.

See also Indigenous Women of the Americas Defenders of Mother Earth Treaty Compact 2015, as they describe their commitment to defend their matriarchal right to protect their community.

As my stewardship improves, the plants and animals teach me more ways to grow through the covenant God made with Abraham. A fellow citizen of Trinidad and Tobago helped me appreciate the covenant in a new way. Tiffanie Drayton wrote a book, *Black American Refugee*, which describes how and why she became a refugee back to Trinidad and Tobago.

Appendix

Countries in Europe have, at one time or another, colonized just about every corner of the globe, either outright or under various designations like "protectorate" or "mandate." This includes the entirety of the Americas and all of Africa save for little Liberia. The Middle East and Asia were divided up as well.

Almost every Corner of the Globe came under European Control. Some countries instead fell under "spheres of influence," in which a European power would declare that country or some part of it subject to their influence, which was a step removed from, but in practice not all that distinct from, conquering it outright. Iran, for example, was divided between British and Russian spheres of influence, which meant that the European powers owned exclusive rights to Iranian oil and gas in their areas, among other things.

Most of the areas under spheres of influence were politically dominated by the British, who ruled through proxies: Afghanistan (which also endured Russian influence), Bhutan, and Nepal. Mongolia was effectively a proxy state of the Soviet Union for much of the Cold War.

142

Acknowledgements

This manuscript presents the core philosophy and spiritual foundation of my first book, *Observing Earth's Lifestyle*. It is much shorter and more concise, thanks to the enormous support and assistance of Rev. Lydia Huttar Brown, a dear friend of my wife Kathryn and me. Lydia is from Minnesota and travels with her husband, Mark, and a team of teachers, who conduct a training program in a Mayan community in Belize, where we first met.

Historian Bob Barde is a colleague of Kathy with whom she worked at the University of California, Berkeley and has studied and written department documents on Asian migration into the Western USA.

Rev. Richard Singleton is the person who first introduced me to the Doctrine of Discovery, the central theme of the manuscript. Along the way he has helped me clarify many early impressions of the Jesus lifestyle. His wife, Sharron, is a poet and avid gardener, who has helped me appreciate the persistent vitality of God's Holy Temple outdoors.

Rev. Justin Cannon is the organizer of Holy Hikes, a monthly Eucharist celebrated outdoors in the San Francisco Bay Area. The Holy Hikes sermons are shared reflections of God speaking to us through personal meditations related to one's sense of the environment at that point on the hike.

The late Sr. Barbara Hazzard was my spiritual director for over twenty years at the Hesed Community in Oakland, California. She continued directing much of my spiritual growth through my first few years in Belize.

Rev. Dr. Kwasi Thornell has led me through a unique appreciation for those aspects of the Jesus lifestyle that teach his disciples to build dependable and reliable community. Rev. Thornell is now one of the most respected and experienced leaders in the Episcopal Church. He has been appointed by the Bishop of the Diocese of Miami as his Deputy for Special Ministries to work in anti-racism and reconciliation.

As I explore the Jesus lifestyle, I seek to follow Jesus as a faithful disciple. I realize that my emphasis has been influenced by a retreat I attended at Adelynrood Conference Center, which was led by then Bishop Curry in 2012. Now the Presiding Bishop of the Episcopal Church of the USA, he had used the Gospel of Matthew to highlight how, through God all things are possible.

In addition, I must remember the late Dr. Clarence Jackson, an Education Psychologist for the State of California. We became close friends, as he impressed on me that my teaching had to motivate me to learn from my students. At the community college level my students taught me unique insights from their own life experience.

Finally, I want to thank James Schinnerer and Jennifer Holbrook, acknowledging their immense assistance in editing my manuscript, giving it needed clarity and direction.

Bibliography

Aldredge-Clanton, Jann. *In Search of the Christ-Sophia*. Fort Worth, Texas: Eakin Press, 1995, 2004.

Alexander, Michelle. *The New Jim Crow*. New York: The New Press, 2012.

Pope Alexander VI, (1431-1503). *Demarcation bull.*, granting Spain possession of lands discovered by Columbus.

Anderson, Alita. *On the Other Side: African Americans Tell of Healing*. Louisville, Kentucky: Westminster John Knox Press, 2001.

Anderson, Carol. *Bourgeois Radicals: The NAACP and the Struggle for Colonial Liberation 1941-1960*. New York: Cambridge University Press, December 2014.

Anthony, Carl, and M. Paloma Pavel. *Breakthrough Communities*. Berkeley, CA: Ecology Center, 2012.

Armstrong, Karen. *A History of God: The 4,000 year Quest of Judaism, Christianity and Islam*. New York: Random House, 1993.

Awatisgi, Nvnehi (Jim PathFinder Ewing). *Finding Sanctuary in Nature: Simple Ceremonies in the Native American Tradition for Healing Yourself and Others*. Forres, Scotland: Findhorn Press, 2007.

Baker, Dori Grinenko, editor. *Greenhouses of Hope: Congregations Growing Young Leaders Who Will Change the World*. Herndon, Virginia: The Alban Institute, 2010.

Ball, Edward. *Slaves in the Family*. New York: Farrar, Straus and Giroux, 1998.

Bass, Diana Butler. *Christianity After Religion*. New York, New York: HarperOne, Harper Collins Publishers, 2012.

Barrett, Samuel A., and Edward W. Gifford. *Indian Life of the Yosemite Region: Miwok Material Culture*, Bulletin of the Milwaukee Public Museum, volume 2, no.4 March 1933.

Battle, Michael. *Reconciliation: The Ubuntu Theology of Desmond Tutu*. Cleveland, Ohio: The Pilgrim Press, 1997.

Behrman, Richard E., editor. *The Future of Children, Long-Term Outcomes of Early Childhood Programs*. Center for the Future of Children, 1995.

Benor, Daniel, and James Q. Harrison. *Agricultural Extension: the Training and Visit System*, for the World Bank, May 1977.

Berry, Thomas. *The Sacred Universe*. New York, New York: Columbia University Press, 2009.

Bolland, O. Nigel. *Struggle for Freedom, Essays on Slavery, Colonialism and Culture in the Caribbean and Central America*. The Angelus Press, Ian Randle Publishers Ltd., 1997.

Borg, Marcus J. *Meeting Jesus Again for the First Time: The Historical Jesus and the Heart of Contemporary Faith*. New York, New York: Harper Collins Publishers, 1994.

Borg, Marcus J. *The Heart of Christianity: Rediscovering a Life of Faith*. New York, New York: Harper Collins Publishers, 2003.

Borg, Marcus J. *Jesus: Uncovering the Life, Teachings and Relevance of a Religious Revolutionary*. New York, New York: Harper Collins Publishers, 2006.

Borg, Marcus J., and John Dominic Crossan. *The Last Week: What the Gospels Really Teach About Jesus's Final Days in Jerusalem*. New York, New York: Harper Collins Publishers, 2006.

Bourgeault, Cynthia. *The Wisdom Jesus: Transforming Heart and Mind – A New Perspective on Christ and His Message*. Boston, Massachusetts: Shambhala Publications, Inc., 2008.

Bourgeault, Cynthia. *The Wisdom Way of Knowing: Reclaiming an Ancient Tradition to Awaken the Heart*. San Francisco, California: Jossey-Bass, 2003.

Brower, David. *Let the Mountains Talk, Let the Rivers Run.* 2nd edition. New York, NY: New Society Publishers, 2000.

Brower, Michael, and Warren Leon. *The Consumer's Guide to Effective Environmental Choices: Practical Advice from The Union of Concerned Scientists.* New York, New York: Three Rivers Press, Random House, Inc., 1999.

Brown, Robert McAfee, and Sydney Thomson Brown. *A Cry For Justice: The Churches and Synagogues Speak.* Mahwah, New Jersey: Paulist Press, 1989.

Carter, Forrest. *The Education of Little Tree.* Albuquerque, New Mexico: University of New Mexico Press, 1976.

Charleston, Steven. *The Four Vision Quests of Jesus.* New York, New York: Morehouse Publishing, Inc., 2015.

Chilton, Bruce. *Rabbi Jesus: An Intimate Biography, The Jewish Life and Teachings That Inspired Christianity.* New York, New York: An Image Book, Doubleday, Random House, Inc., 2000.

Chittister, Joan. *God's Tender Mercy: Reflections on Forgiveness.* New London, Connecticut: Twenty-Third Publications, 2010.

Chittister, Joan. *The Rule of Benedict: A Spirituality for the 21st Century.* 2nd edition. New York: The Crossroad Publishing Company, 2010.

Chittister, Joan. *The Time is Now: A Call to Uncommon Courage*. New York: Convergent Books, a division of Penguin Random House LLC, 2019.

Chodron, Pema. *When Things Fall Apart: Heart Advice for Difficult Times*. 1997. Boston, Massachusetts: Shambhala Publications, Inc., 1997.

The Dalai Lama, His Holiness and Archbishop Desmond Tutu, in collaboration with Douglas Abrams. *The Book of Joy: Lasting Happiness in a Changing World*. New York, New York: Avery, an imprint of Penguin Random House, 2016.

Davis, Devra. *When Smoke Ran Like Water: Tales of Environmental Deception and the Battle Against Pollution*. New York, New York: Basic Books, Perseus Books Group, 2002.

Delio, Ilie, Keith Douglass Warner, and Pamela Wood. *Care For Creation: A Franciscan Spirituality of the Earth*. Cincinnati, Ohio: St. Anthony Messenger Press, 2008.

Diamond, Jared. *Guns, Germs, and Steel: The Fates of Human Societies*. New York, New York: W.W. Norton, 1997.

Diamond, Jared. *Collapse: How Societies Choose to Fail or Succeed*. New York, New York: Penguin, 2005.

Diamond, Jared. *The World Until Yesterday: What Can We Learn From Traditional Societies?* New York, New York: Viking Press, 2012.

Dillard, Annie. *Pilgrim at Tinker Creek*. New York, New York: Harper and Row, 1974.

Dozier, Verna J. *The Dream of God: A Call to Return*. Boston, Massachusetts: Cowley Publications, 1991. (Also published by Cowley Press: *The Authority of the Laity*.)

Duhon, David, and Cindy Gebhard. *One Circle: How to Grow a Complete Diet in Less Than 1,000 Square Feet*. Ecology Action, 1985.

Edwards, Andres R. *The Sustainability Revolution, Portrait of a Paradigm Shift*. New Society Publishers, 2005.

Equal Justice Initiative: A History of Racial Injustice, 2021 Calendar, Stop Police Killings, 2020, Montgomery, Alabama, eji.org.

Farmer, Paul. *Pathologies of Power: Health, Human Rights and the New War on the Poor*. 1st edition. Berkeley, California: University of California Press, 2003.

Pope Francis. *Encyclical Letter: Care for Our Common Home*. Proclaimed by Pope Francis at the Vatican, 18 June 2015.

Gargello, Francesca. "El Pueblo Garifuna", Cuadrenos Pedagogicos No. 18, Ministerio de Educacion, Guatemala, 24 de julio de 2002.

Giroux, Henry A. *Hearts of Darkness: Torturing Children in the War on Terror*. Boulder, Colorado: Paradigm Publishers, 2010.

The Green Bible. New Revised Standard Version Bible, Division of Christian Education of the National Council of Churches of Christ in the United States of America. HarperCollins Publishers, 1989.

Grimes Jr., Orville F. *Housing for Low-Income Urban Families, Economics and Policy in the Developing World.* A World Bank Research Project. Baltimore Maryland: Johns Hopkins University Press, 1976.

Grizwold, Eliza. *The Tenth Parallel: Dispatches from the Fault Line Between Christianity and Islam.* New York, New York: Farrar, Straus and Giroux, 2010.

Gushee, David P. "Born in Heresy", Sojourners Magazine, Sept/Oct 2020, Vol. 49 No. 9, sojo.net.

Hacker, Andrew. *Two Nations, Black and White, Separate, Hostile, Unequal.* 1st Edition. New York, New York: Charles Scribner's Sons, 1992.

Hawken, Paul. *Blessed Unrest: How the Largest Movement In the World Came Into Being* and *Why No One Saw it Coming.* New York, New York: Viking Press, 2007.

Ilibagiza, Immaculee. *Left to Tell: Discovering God Amidst the Rwandan Holocaust.* Carlsbad, California: Hay House, Inc., 2006.

Jayaraman, Saru. *Behind The Kitchen Door.* Ithaca, New York: Cornell University Press, 2013.

Jeavons, John. *How to Grow More Vegetables*. 3rd edition. Ecology Action of the Mid-Peninsula. Berkeley, California: 10 Speed Press, 1982.

Jones, Shirley Ann, editor. *Simply Living: The Spirit of the Indigenous People*. Novato, California: New World Library, 1999.

Kristof, Nicholas D., and Sheryl WuDunn. *Half the Sky: Turning Oppression into Opportunity for Women Worldwide*. New York, New York: Alfred A. Knopf, 2009.

Kroeber, Theodora. *Ishi in Two Worlds*. Berkeley, California: University of California Press, 1961, 1976.

Leiva, Julio Leiva. *El Terco Deseo de Crea: Un Mejor Mañana*. Bilingual Edition. San Salvador, El Salvador, C.A.: Editorial Molino DeViento, 2005.

Mails, Thomas E. *The Mystic Warriors of the Plains*. Mallard Press, 1991.

Mann, Charles C. *1491: New Revelations of the Americas Before Columbus*. New York, New York: First Vintage Books, 2006.

Manz, Beatriz. *Paradise in Ashes*. Berkeley, California: University of California Press, 2004.

Margolin, Malcolm. *The Ohlone Way: Indian life in the San Francisco-Monterey Bay Area*. Berkeley, California: Heyday Books, 1978.

Mashable.com. *Wonderworld: A photographic journey of planet Earth.* Mashable.com/2015/04/03/wonderworld-photos-of-earth / April 3, 2015.

Matthew, Iain. *The Impact of God: Soundings from St. John of The Cross.* London: Hodder & Stoughton, a Division of Hodder Headline Ltd., 1995.

McKibben, Bill. *The End of Nature. 1ˢᵗ edition. New York, New York: Random House, 1989.*

McKibben, Bill. <u>*Eaarth*</u>*: Making a life on a tough new planet.* First Edition. New York: Times Books, an imprint of Henry Holt and Co, 2010.

McLaren, Brian D. *The Secret Message of Jesus: Uncovering the Truth that Could Change Everything.* Nashville, Tennessee: W Publishing Group, A Division of Thomas Nelson, Inc., 2006.

McLaren, Brian D. *Everything Must Change: Jesus, Global Crises, and a Revolution of Hope.* Nashville, Tennessee: W Publishing Group, A Division of Thomas Nelson, Inc., 2007.

Meyer, Marvin W. *The Secret Teachings of Jesus: Four Gnostic Gospels.* 1ˢᵗ edition. New York, New York: Vintage Books, a Division of Random House, 1984.

MSF Treating People on the Move, Doctors Without Borders MSF Report, (Medecins Sans Frontierres), *Alert*, Responding to the Global Refugee Crisis, Fall 2017, vol 18, no. 3.

Murthy, Vivek. *Together: The Healing Power of Human Connection in a Sometimes Lonely World*. New York, New York: HarperCollins Publishers, 2020.

Myers, Bryant L. *Walking with the Poor: Principles and Practices of Transformational Development*. Maryknoll, New York: Orbis Books, 1999.

Nazario, Sonia. *Enrique's Journey*. New York, New York: Random House Trade Paperback, 2006.

The New English Bible, Oxford Study Edition. Oxford University Press, 1961.

Newcomb, Steve. *Five Hundred Years of Injustice: The Legacy of Fifteenth Century Religious Prejudice*, 1992.

Pope Nicholas V: papal bull Dum Diversas, 18 June 1452, issued to King Alfonso V of Portugal the bull Romanus Pontifcx, which became the Doctrine of Discovery.

Pagels, Elaine. *Beyond Belief: The Secret Gospel of Thomas*. New York, New York: Random House, New York, 2003.

Paintner, Christine Valters. *Desert Fathers and Mothers: Early Christian Wisdom Sayings Annotated & Explained*. 1st edition. Woodstock, Vermont: SkyLight Paths Publishing, 2012.

Paul, Daniel N. Doctrine of Discovery: the Doctrines Decreed by Roman Catholic Popes. Source: *First Nations History*, Third Edition, 2007.

Pavel, M. Paloma. *Breakthrough Communities: Sustainability and Justice in the Next American Metropolis*. 1st edition. Cambridge, Massachusetts: MIT Press, 2009.

Reynolds, Edward. *Stand the Storm: a History of the Atlantic Slave Trade*. 1st edition. London: Allison and Busby, Ltd., 1985.

Romain, David L. *Observing Earth's Lifestyle, Considering the Value of Earth Stewardship in Environmental Protection*, 2017.

Savary, Louis M. *The New Spiritual Exercises, In the Spirit of Pierre Teilhard de Chardin*. 1st edition. Mahwah, New Jersey: Paulist Press, 2010.

Sen, Amartya. *Poverty and Famines: An Essay on Entitlement and Deprivation*. Oxford: Clarendon Press. 1981.

Shimer, Porter. *Healing Secrets of the Native Americans*. New York, New York: Black Dog and Leventhal Publishers, 2004.

Sierra Club Books of San Francisco. *Endangered Peoples*. Text copyright: Art Davidson, 1993. Photograph copyright: Art Wolfe and John Isaac, 1993.

Singleton, Richard O. *The Last Words of the Resurrected Christ*. Winona, Minnesota: Saint Mary's Press, 1997.

Somé, Malidoma Patrice. *Of Water and The Spirit: Ritual, Magic and Invitation in the Life of an African Shaman.* New York, New York: Penguin Books, 1995.

Somé, Sobonfu. *The Spirit of Intimacy: Ancient Teachings in the Ways of Relationships.* 1st edition. Berkeley, California: Berkeley Hills Books, 1997.

Somé, Sobonfu. *Welcoming Spirit Home: Ancient African Teachings to Celebrate Children and Community.* Novato, California: New World Library, 1999.

Spellers, Stephanie. *Radical Welcome: Embracing God, The Other, and the Spirit of Transformation.* New York, New York: Church Publishing, Incorporated, 2006.

Stevenson, Bryan. *Just Mercy.* New York, New York: Spiegel and Grau, an imprint of Penguin Random House, L.L.C., 2014.

Still, William. *The Underground Railroad* (Ebony Classics). Chicago, Illinois: Johnson Publishing Company, 1970.

Swan, Michael. "Doctrine of Discovery First Repudiated in 1537", writing for The Catholic Register, October 2, 2014.

Taylor, Barbara Brown. *An Altar in the World: A Geography of Faith.* 1st edition. New York, New York: Harper Collins and HarperOne, 2009.

Taylor, Barbara Brown. *Learning to Walk in the Dark.* 1st edition. New York, New York: Harper Collins and HarperOne, 2014.

Thurman, Howard. *Jesus and the Disinherited*. Boston, Massachusetts: Beacon Press Books, 1976.

Wallis, Jim. *On God's Side: What Religion Forgets and Politics hasn't Learned About Serving the Common Good*. Grand Rapids, Michigan: Brazos Press, Baker Publishing Group, 2013.

Wallis, Jim. *America's Original Sin: Racism, White Privilege and the Bridge to a New America*. Grand Rapids, Michigan: Brazos Press, Baker Publishing Group, 2016.

Weart, Spencer. *The Discovery of Global Warming*. Harvard University Press, 2003.

West, Cornel. *Restoring Hope: Conversations on the Future of Black America*. Boston, Massachusetts: Beacon Press, 1997.

Williams, Juan. *Eyes on the Prize: America's Civil Rights Years, 1954-1965*. New York, New York: Viking, Blackside, Inc., 1987.

Wink, Walter. *Engaging the Powers: Discernment and Resistance in a World of Domination*. Minneapolis, Minnesota: Fortress Press, 1992.